First World War
and Army of Occupation
War Diary
France, Belgium and Germany

3 CAVALRY DIVISION
Headquarters, Branches and Services
General Staff Appendices to 1141
1 January 1918 - 22 January 1918

WO95/1142/4

The Naval & Military Press Ltd
www.nmarchive.com
Published in association with The National Archives

Published by

The Naval & Military Press Ltd

Unit 10 Ridgewood Industrial Park,

Uckfield, East Sussex,

TN22 5QE England

Tel: +44 (0) 1825 749494

www.naval-military-press.com

www.nmarchive.com

This diary has been reprinted in facsimile from the original. Any imperfections are inevitably reproduced and the quality may fall short of modern type and cartographic standards.

© Crown Copyright
Images reproduced by permission of The National Archives, London, England, 2015.

Contents

Document type	Place/Title	Date From	Date To
Heading	3rd Cavalry Division Intelligence Summary Jan 1918 Dec 1918.		
Miscellaneous	Summary Of Intelligence, No. 11 Appendix 1	01/01/1918	01/01/1918
Miscellaneous	Summary Of Intelligence, No. 12. Appendix 1	02/01/1918	02/01/1918
Miscellaneous	Summary Of Intelligence, No. 13. Appendix 1	03/01/1918	03/01/1918
Miscellaneous	Annexe To Intelligence Summary, No. 13.		
Miscellaneous	Summary Of Intelligence, No. 14. Appendix 1	04/01/1918	04/01/1918
Miscellaneous	Summary Of Intelligence, No. 15. Appendix 1	05/01/1918	05/01/1918
Miscellaneous	Summary Of Intelligence, No. 16. Appendix 1	06/01/1918	06/01/1918
Miscellaneous	Summary Of Intelligence, No. 17. Appendix 1	07/01/1918	07/01/1918
Miscellaneous	Summary Of Intelligence, No. 18. Appendix 1	08/01/1918	08/01/1918
Miscellaneous	Morning Communique-8th.		
Miscellaneous	Summary Of Intelligence No. 10. Appendix 1		
Miscellaneous	Summary Of Intelligence No. 20. Appendix 1	10/01/1918	10/01/1918
Miscellaneous	Summary Of Intelligence No. 21. Appendix 1	11/01/1918	11/01/1918
Miscellaneous	Summary Of Intelligence No. 22. Appendix 1	12/01/1918	12/01/1918
Miscellaneous	Summary Of Intelligence No. 23. Appendix 1	13/01/1918	13/01/1918
Miscellaneous	Summary Of Intelligence No. 24. Appendix 1	14/01/1918	14/01/1918
Miscellaneous	Summary Of Intelligence No. 25. Appendix 1	15/01/1918	15/01/1918
Miscellaneous	Summary Of Intelligence No. 26. Appendix 1	16/01/1918	16/01/1918
Miscellaneous	Summary Of Intelligence No. 27. Appendix 1	17/01/1918	17/01/1918
Miscellaneous	Summary Of Intelligence No. 28. Appendix 1	18/01/1918	18/01/1918
Miscellaneous	Summary Of Intelligence No. 29. Appendix 1	19/01/1918	19/01/1918
Miscellaneous	Summary Of Intelligence No. 30. Appendix 1	20/01/1918	20/01/1918
Miscellaneous	Summary Of Intelligence No. 31. Appendix 1	21/01/1918	21/01/1918
Miscellaneous	Summary Of Intelligence No. 32. Appendix 1	22/01/1918	22/01/1918
Miscellaneous	3rd Dismounted Division. A.D.M.D. Appendix 2	07/01/1918	07/01/1918
Miscellaneous	3rd Dismounted Division. Appendix 3	05/01/1918	05/01/1918
Miscellaneous	March Tables.		
Operation(al) Order(s)	Dismounted Division Order No. 2. Appendix 4	10/01/1918	10/01/1918
Miscellaneous	Table Of Reliefs Issued With Dismounted Division Order. No. 2		
Operation(al) Order(s)	Warning Order. Appendix 5	10/01/1918	10/01/1918
Miscellaneous	2nd Dismounted Division. Appendix 6	12/01/1918	12/01/1918
Operation(al) Order(s)	Dismounted Divisions Order No. 3. Appendix 4	13/01/1918	13/01/1918
Miscellaneous	Table "A" Issued Dismounted Division Order No. 3.		
Miscellaneous	Table "B" Issued With Dismounted Division Order No. 3.		
Miscellaneous	6th Cavalry Brigade. Appendix 8	16/01/1918	16/01/1918
Miscellaneous	Table Of Reliefs Of 3rd Cavalry Pioneer Regiment, Issued With Dismounted Divisions G. 842/6 Dated 18.1.18		
Miscellaneous	2nd Dismounted Division. A.D.V.S. Appendix 9	20/01/1918	20/01/1918
Miscellaneous	March Table.		
Miscellaneous	Warning Order. Appendix 10	21/01/1918	21/01/1918
Operation(al) Order(s)	3rd. Cavalry Division Order No. 14. Appendix 11	25/01/1918	25/01/1918
Miscellaneous	March Table Issued With 3rd. Cavalry Division Order No. 14.		

3rd Cavalry Division

Intelligence Summaries

Jan. 1918 –
Dec. 1918.

Appendix 1

CONFIDENTIAL.　　SUMMARY OF INTELLIGENCE, No.11.

H.Q., DISMOUNTED DIVISIONS.

for 24 hours ending 8.0 a.m. 1/1/18.

=*=*=*=*=*=*=*=*=*=*=*=*=*=*=*=*=

1. OPERATIONS.

   (a) Our Patrols.

   A patrol reconnoitred ANGLE BANK, BOISEVILLE WOOD and DOG'S LEG, and reported them clear of the enemy.

   (b) Our M.G's.

   One of our M.G. Groups registered S.O.S. barrage at 10.0 p.m.

2. HOSTILE ATTITUDE AND ACTIVITY.

   (a) Artillery.

   10.15 - 11.20 a.m.　30 7.7's fired into L.12.a. and G.7.b. from direction of BELLICOURT.
   11.30 a.m.　Slight shelling of L.30.c.
   　　　　　　12 rounds H.E. fell close to DRAGOON POST.
   　　　　　　4 "duds" fired into PONTRU area.

   (b) Movement.

   The usual movement of individuals observed throughout the day, along the enemy's front system, especially to and from SKIN TRENCH (G.8) and in G.20 and G.27.
   　　　　Continual movement also reported during the day between DIAMOND COPSE and SENTINEL RIDGE.
   　　　　　　　See also para.5 below.

   10.30 a.m.　Several men entered BILLIARD COPSE from every direction.
   11.15 a.m.　16 men seen on road in G.34.c. - disappeared into house about G.34.b.3.2.
   11.17 a.m.　3 men repair screens on CHOPPER RAVINE road.
   2.10 p.m.　Small working party at SWAN WORK dispersed by our artillery.
   3.25 p.m.　10 men left trench at G.20.b.6.2., disappearing in sunk road about G.20.b.1.3. They returned to trench at 3.40 p.m.
   3.55 p.m.　6 men carrying food containers about G.8.a.9.4.

   (c) Aviation.

   3.15 p.m.　1 E.A. crossed our lines between TUMULUS and R. l'OMIGNON, dropping 2 bombs, one of which did not explode. No damage done.

3. HOSTILE DEFENCES.

   Work. Parties of 2 - 4 men each were seen digging at various points in the enemy's front trenches, probably engaged on upkeep of trenches.
   2 men were seen digging in crater at G.20.d.4.5. at 8.50 a.m. Another man, in long cloak, came up and talked to them for a few minutes.

4. MISCELLANEOUS.

   A patrol from the centre of our line brought in a red paper balloon. It is of German manufacture and it's dimensions are as follows: length 1' 6", circumference 7', tail 2' 6" long.

   .... She

The Division on our right report 2 similar balloons falling in their lines.

5. SPECIAL REPORT.

The following enemy movement, observed on each of the last 3 mornings, appears to be of special interest:

7.20 a.m. 29th. 80-90 men went in single file up SKIN TRENCH from G.8.a.5.6. in Northerly direction, and disappeared from view about G.2.c.5.0. Only heads and shoulders seen.

8.5 a.m. 30th. 80-90 men seen going down SKIN TRENCH from G.8.a. central, where they seemed to turn into what appears to be a C.T. leading into sunken road about G.8.d.7.6.

8.10 a.m. 40 men, in small parties, armed and carrying equipment, left SKIN TRENCH about G.8.a.5.6. and proceeded towards QUARRY RAVINE.

This movement was at first thought to indicate the completion of a local relief. But it's recurrence tends to show that a large part of the enemy's front line garrison is withdrawn after daylight.

                                                       Captain,

                                     G.S., Dismounted Divisions.

1st January, 1918.

NEWS. (From Cav. Corps wire, 10.35 a.m.)

"As result of counter-attacks in which our troops captured prisoners and M.G's, we have regained more important part of positions lost on 30th ult., but enemy still retain portion of our front trench in neighbourhood LA VACQUERIE and S. of MARCOING.

"Italian Front; On 30th ult. after careful artillery preparations, French troops successfully stormed enemy's positions between OSTERIA DE MONFENERA and MARANZINE, and captured 44 Officers, 1348 O.R., 60 M.G's, 7 cannons, and large quantity of other material. British artillery and aircraft co-operated.

"Under new Russian peace treaty, war is declared to be at an end and economic relations are to be resumed as early as possible with Germany.

Appendix 1

<u>CONFIDENTIAL.</u>

<u>SUMMARY OF INTELLIGENCE, No. 12.</u>

<u>H.Q., DISMOUNTED DIVISIONS.</u>

for 24 hours ending 8.0 a.m. 2/1/18.

1. <u>OPERATIONS.</u>

   <u>Our Patrols.</u>

   A patrol of 2 Officers and 40 O.R., leaving No. 8 Post at 5.15 p.m. returned to point between Nos. 1 and 2 Posts via ASCENSION WOOD and G.19.a.7.3. at 7.30 p.m. They reported ASCENSION WOOD and Valley to N. clear of enemy.

   ASCENSION WOOD being made good, scouts pushed on to BIG BILL and LITTLE BILL. No signs of any hostile force were seen or heard. A small funk-hole in W.E. corner of ASCENSION WOOD but no signs of occupation since fall of snow. Valley reported clear to G.19.d.7.3.

   A patrol of 1 Officer and 18 O.R. left LONE TREE POST at 10.30 p.m. and returned to DRAGOON POST at 1 a.m. via SOMERVILLE WOOD, DOG'S LEG M.2.b. and ANGLE BANK. They reported everywhere all clear of the enemy.

   A good position was found at M.2.c.9.8. to look down on to FISHERS CRATER. A dozen Very Lights were fired from ELEVEN TREES between 10.30 p.m. and 12.30 a.m.

2. <u>HOSTILE ATTITUDE AND ACTIVITY.</u>

   (b) <u>Movement.</u>

   A certain amount of movement was observed between SKIN TRENCH and QUARRY WOOD.

7.30 a.m.	4 men came from M.5.a.2.7. and disappeared behind building at G.35.c.3.2. Small parties carrying here all day.
8.12 a.m.	8 men left trench at G.20.b.8.0. and disappeared in sunken road at G.21.a.2.5.
8.15 a.m.	6 men on top of trench at G.28.d.2.9. carried timber towards BLACKTOWN.
9.0 a.m.	4 men carrying timber at G.35.c.4.4.
9.30 a.m.	8 men left screens at G.35.b.1.8. and disappeared in BULLET COPSE.
11.0 a.m.	Small working party was observed at G.8.c.9.9. SKIN TRENCH, apparently clearing the trench.
11.10 a.m.	5 men from BILLIARD COPSE get in trench at G.23.c.7.1.
1.0 p.m.	9 men left BILLIARD COPSE, entering trench at G.23.c.7.1.
1.30 p.m.	7 men carrying hurdles in G.35.c.7.4.
2.45 p.m.	4 men digging at G.35.c.4.4.

   (c) <u>Aviation.</u> Nothing to report.

(Sd) W.P. BROWNE,
Captain,

2nd January, 1918.

G.S., Dismounted Divisions.

Appendix 1

CONFIDENTIAL.

SUMMARY OF INTELLIGENCE, No. 13.

H.Q., DISMOUNTED DIVISIONS.

for 24 hours ending 6.0 a.m. 3/1/18.

1. **OPERATIONS.**

   (a) *Our Patrols.*

   A patrol of 1 Officer and 30 O.R. reconnoitred BUISSON RIDGE and the valley running S. to ASCENSION WOOD. The patrol reported as follows:-
   - (i) L.P. at G.19.d.8.8. has not been used since snow fell. It consists of 8 separate holes, facing S.W. 3 coils of wire observed near these holes.
   - (ii) Trees on BUISSON RIDGE clear of enemy. No tracks seen there. Small trench about G.19.b.70.85. appeared unused.
   - (iii) Small trench, full of snow, found about G.19.d.5.9.
   - (iv) No tracks found in Valley in G.19.d.

   DOG'S LEG and MAX WOOD were patrolled and reported clear. Our usual protective patrols visited SOMERVILLE WOOD and ANGLE BANK every 5 hours.

   2 small patrols went up the 2 old saps in G.7.b. leading from RAILWAY TRENCH to BANK TRENCH. Both saps are reported to be blocked 40 yards from our trench. Neither sap was occupied by the enemy. The southern patrol was fired on, when they reached the enemy's wire, by M.G's - thought to be located about G.7.b.95.80.

   (b) *Our M.G's and T.M's.*

   At 4.0 p.m., 7.0 p.m. and 8.15 p.m. our M.G's fired dropping fire on to FARM TRENCH between G.14.c.40.75 and G.14.c.55.55.
   Our T.M's fired a few bursts on BANK TRENCH during the night.

2. **HOSTILE ATTITUDE AND ACTIVITY.**

   (a) *Artillery.*

   ONION LANE intermittently shelled with 4.2's during morning.
   20 T.M. bombs fired into VILLERET and MAXIM LANE between 9.30 a.m. and noon.
   Slight shelling of the TUMULUS and of G.25.d. in the afternoon.

   (b) *Movement.*

   8.20 a.m. 9 men working behind ROSE TRENCH, wheeling earth away in barrows.
   8.30 a.m. 10 men, with arms and equipment, entered SKIN TRENCH about G.8.c.9.6.
   8.45 a.m. 1 man seen W. of LITTLE BILL at G.20.c.2.5. in what is thought to be a new L.P.
   9.10 a.m. 3 men working on wire W. of SWAN WORK. Fired on by Officer from DRAGOON POST and dispersed - one man believed hit.
   9.30 a.m. Armed party of 50 men going N. up PEN TRENCH.
   9.40 a.m. Armed party (about 30 strong) moving S.E. from BILLIARD COPSE into trench in G.29.
   10.10 a.m. 8 men going N.E. from G.28.d.1.1.
   10.35 a.m. 5 men started digging in SWAN WORK - dispersed by our artillery.
   10.50 a.m. 12 men moving up C.T. from G.33.d.5.0. towards BIG BEAR.

   (c) *Aviation.* E.A. activity nil.

W. Browne
Captain,
G.S., Dismounted Divisions.

3rd January, 1918.

ANNEXE TO INTELLIGENCE SUMMARY, No. 13.

1. ACCOUNT OF AN OFFICER'S PATROL ON FRONT OF DIVISION ON OUR LEFT, ON NIGHT 30th/31st.

At 6.15 p.m. an Officer and 1 O.R. went along a sap under the enemy's wire and entered the enemy's trench at about G.7.a.9.9.
20 yards away, 5 of the enemy were seen to leave the trench and go away over the open.
Patrol entered a dugout and found 8 loaded rifles, a box of tools (for Minenwerfer), 12 boxes of fuzes, 5 bayonets and various other articles. A portion of this material was brought back to our lines. The patrol then made two more journeys to the dugout and brought the remainder of the booty.
Some papers were also secured, one of which was addressed to an N.C.O. of the 35th Minenwerfer Coy. (35th Division, which was in this Sector from July to October, 1917).
Half an hour later the enemy fired Very Lights and a machine gun from this point.

2. MORNING COMMUNIQUE, 3rd JAN.

"Heavy hostile barrage put down near LEMPIRE 4.20 - 4.40 a.m. Quiet night on rest of Army front. Hostile raids repulsed neighbourhood LENS, MENIN Road and PASSCHENDAELE. Prisoners taken from enemy raiding parties in No Man's Land.
"ITALIAN Front: Austrians compelled to forsake their large bridge-head at LENSON Loop of PIAVE by infantry and artillery attack.
"PALESTINE: Advance of British troops continues. During first 3 days 750 prisoners captured and 1,000 enemy dead counted.
"RUSSIAN: Whole COSSACK population women and men mobilised for civil war. Thousands officers regular Army flocking to KALEDIN. ALEXANDROVITCH occupied by Cossacks without resistance."

3. BRITISH CAPTURES ON WESTERN FRONT IN 1917.

British captures on the Western Front in 1917 alone are as under:-

    74,349 German prisoners.
       542 Guns (all calibres).
       847 T.M's.
     2,422 M.G's.

Appendix 1

CONFIDENTIAL. SUMMARY OF INTELLIGENCE, No. 14.

H.Q., DISMOUNTED DIVISION.

For 24 hours ending 3.0 a.m. 4/1/18.

1. **OPERATIONS.**

   (a) *Our Patrols.*

   A patrol of 2 Officers and 40 O.R., who reconnoitred BIG BILL and LITTLE BILL, engaged an enemy patrol in the valley G.19.d. When our patrol was at about G.19.d.7.3., they heard voices coming from the North. They advanced 100 yards and heard an enemy patrol approaching, which consisted of 3 columns of about 20 each, with another party in support. Our scouts then opened fire and the enemy patrol retired, after firing a few rounds.

   The following localities were, also, reconnoitred and reported clear: FISHER'S CRATER, MAX WOOD, DOG'S LEG, SOMERVILLE WOOD and ANGLE BANK.

   (b) *Our M.G's and T.M's.*

   At 7.0 p.m. and at 9.0 p.m., our M.G's fired 2,000 rounds harassing fire at BREW LANE (G.14.d.) and PEARL WOOD.
   2 of our T.M's fired several rounds on the M.G. located at G.7.b.95.30. and on G.8.a.1.2. (BANK TRENCH), where new work had been observed.

   (c) *Our Hotchkiss Rifles.*

   An enemy wiring party, heard in front of BANK TRENCH (about G.7.b.8.8.) at 11.30 p.m., was engaged by our H.R's and dispersed.

2. **HOSTILE ATTITUDE AND ACTIVITY.**

   (a) *Artillery.*

   Generally quiet.

   10.40 - 11.40 a.m.   20 4.2's fired into MAXIM LANE and FARM SUPPORT. Direction NAUROY.
   1.20 p.m.   9 7.7's fell in VILLERET LANE - direction: NAUROY. Same locality shelled during evening with 18 4.2's.
   3.30 - 4.15 p.m.   30 5.9's fell round the TUMULUS - a large number were blind.

   Intermittent shelling of the OMIGNON Valley, (particularly MAISSEMY) is reported.
   During the evening of the 2nd, about 200 5.9's fell in vicinity of TEMPLEUX.

   (b) *Enemy M.G's.*

   At 11.45 p.m. our wiring party in front of RAILWAY TRENCH were driven in by enemy's M.G. fire.

   (c) *Movement.*

   8.40 a.m.   20 men left trench at G.14.a.5.9., disappearing into QUARRY WOOD.

   ....11.45 a.m.

-2-

11.45 a.m.	12 men filed out of NIGGER COPSE and moved up C.T. towards Canal.
12.40 p.m.	6 men entered C.T. at G.20.b.7.7.
1.45 p.m.	3 men walking along parapet of OMOTO TRENCH.
3.40 p.m.	Earth being thrown up from BANK TRENCH at G.8.c.2.2.

(c) Aviation.

9.0 a.m.	1 E.A. flew over PONTRUET but was driven off by A.A. and M.G. fire.
11.5 a.m.	4 E.A., flying high from N.E. towards HARGICOURT, driven off by A.A. fire.
11.20 a.m.	1 E.A. flew over the right of our line towards VADENCOURT, under A.A. fire.
2.10 p.m.	5 E.A. flew high over the left of our line.
3.30 p.m.	3 E.A. flew over PRIEL FARM POSTS, very high up, and retired N.E. under A.A. fire.

2 hostile balloons were up nearly all day, one about NAUROY, the other near MAGNY-la-FOSSE.

3. HOSTILE DEFENCES.

Small trip wire about 1' high observed on S. side of ELEVEN TREES. Fresh earth seen at about G.28.b.1.5., on parapet of trench. (See also Para. 4.)

4. ENEMY TRENCHES NOT ENTERED ON NAUROY SHEET.

The following trenches have been dug since the NAUROY Sheet was published. Maps showing these lines have been circulated to Intelligence Officers in the line.

(i) From G.2.c.10.30 to G.2.c.70.35.
(ii) " G.8.a.85.20 " G.8.c.20.85.
(iii) " G.8.d.65.45 " G.15.a.3.9.
(iv) " G.14.d.25.95 " G.14.d.7.6.
(v) " G.15.d.3.3. " G.22.c.1.8.
(vi) " G.22.c.2.4. - G.22.c.1.0. - 28.a.5.5. - G.28.b.05.55.
(vii) " G.34.b.1.7. to G.34.c.3.5.

Air photos have confirmed the reports of our observers with regard to trenches in (ii) and (vii) above.

5. MISCELLANEOUS.

A red paper balloon was picked up in PIEUMEL WOOD yesterday afternoon. It is similar to that reported in Summary No.11, para.4. A small electric battery, with a small bulb connected, was attached at the end of the tail.

The balloon recently found in our back area, also, had an electric battery and bulb attached.

Captain,
G.S., Dismounted Divisions.

4th January, 1918.

Appendix 1

CONFIDENTIAL.

SUMMARY OF INTELLIGENCE, No. 15.

H.Q., DISMOUNTED DIVISIONS.

for 24 hours ending 6.0 a.m. 5/1/18.
=*=*=*=*=*=*=*=*=*=*=*=*=*=*=*=*=*=

1. OPERATIONS.

   (a) Our Patrols.

   Owing to the crispness of the frozen snow, movement could be heard a long way off.

   (i) A patrol of 2 Officers and 40 O.R. reconnoitred ASCENSION WOOD and reported it clear of the enemy. No tracks seen in the snow.

   (ii) The ground in G.19.b. was also reconnoitred and no signs of the enemy were seen.

   (iii) A patrol of 2 Officers and 40 O.R. reconnoitred ANGLE BANK, SOMERVILLE WOOD, DOG'S LEG, MAX WOOD and FISHERS CRATER. No enemy encountered but fresh tracks of about 20 men were found leading from MAX WOOD to FISHERS CRATER.

   (iv) An Officer's patrol reconnoitred the little trenches at L.18.a.7.0. and G.13.b.2.1., which do not appear to have been occupied for some time.

   (v) An Officer's patrol went out to reconnoitre enemy's wire at G.8.a.1.2. and to ascertain if enemy holds BANK TRENCH here. Wire is reported to be 15' wide; no gap could be found. An enemy working party was reported about G.8.a.1.1.

   (b) Enemy Patrols.

   One of our patrols heard an enemy patrol moving between BIG and LITTLE BILL.

   (c) Our M.G's.

   From 6.0 p.m. to 8.0 p.m. our M.G's fired 2,000 rounds at each of the following targets.
   BUISSON GAULAINE FARM.
   Track from DIAMOND COPSE to BUCKSHOT RAVINE.
   C.T. from G.20.a.8.9. to G.20.b.6.7.

2. HOSTILE ATTITUDE AND ACTIVITY.

   (a) Artillery.

   Right Sector very quiet all day.

   10.20 a.m. 30 4.2's fell about G.13.b.0.6., including 6 direct hits on MER TRENCH.
   3.10 p.m.   30 4.2's fell near VILLERET LANE L.12.c.8.0.
   3.20 p.m.   11 5.9's "   "   L.12.a.7.1.

   (b) Enemy T.M's.

   9.45 a.m.   T.M. bombs fired into G.7.d.4.0. from direction of L.14.central.

   (c) Movement.

   Visibility very bad all day owing to thick mist.
   Small party standing on parapet in G.14.c. were dispersed by one of our H.R's.

.....(1)

(d) Aviation.

2.40 p.m.   1 E.A. flew high over TUMULUS, PONTRU, COOKER'S QUARRY and ELEVEN TREES, and was then driven off by A.A. fire.
2.50 p.m.   2 E.A. flew over PONTRU, about 1,000 feet up - engaged by A.A. fire.
3.0 p.m.   2 E.A. flew over centre sector very high - driven off by A.A. fire and 1 machine reported to fall behind enemy's lines.
3.15 p.m.   2 E.A. flew very high over ASCENSION FARM.

3. MORNING COMMUNIQUE.

"At next meeting of peace conference Russian delegates will propose immediate evacuation of occupied territory in RUSSIA by German and Austrian troops, and until matter settled they will refuse discuss other terms of peace.

"On night 3rd/4th successful air raids were carried out on factories and railway communications in vicinity of METZ.

"General ALLENBY reports further advance of part of his line N. of JERUSALEM for distance of over a mile."

5th January, 1918.

Captain,
G.S., Dismounted Divisions.

CONFIDENTIAL.

SUMMARY OF INTELLIGENCE, No. 18.

H.Q., DISMOUNTED DIVISIONS.

For 24 hours ending 6.0 a.m. 6/1/18.

1. OPERATIONS.

   Patrols.

   A patrol of 2 Officers and 60 O.R. reconnoitred the L.P. in G.19.d.85.85 and LITTLE BILL, remaining in the N.W. corner of LITTLE BILL for 30 minutes. They sent scouts on a further 300 yards in a N.E. direction. The result of the patrol's reconnaissance was as follows:-

   (i) No enemy patrols seen or heard.

   (ii) Patrol fired on, when about G.19.d.8.8., by M.G's from high ground N. of BUISSON GAULAINE Fm.

   (iii) About 20 new shell holes reported at G.20.d.8.8.

   (iv) Some bombs and 2 sandbags, containing bombs, found at G.19.d.9.8., evidently left by retreating enemy patrol on night 3rd/4th.

   (v) The L.P. on S.E. corner of LITTLE BILL has been used since last snow-fall. "Booby-trap" with a rifle-grenade was found in L.P.

   A patrol of 1 Officer and 18 O.R. went out at 5.0 p.m. from BARRIER POST and formed 2 L.P's in M.2.a. and c., to cover ground between OAK WOOD and FISHER'S CRATER. These L.P's were relieved every hour and were withdrawn at 6.30 a.m. No enemy movement reported.

   1 Officer and 2 O.R. went down the sap from RAILWAY TRENCH at G.7.b.7.2. 50 yards down the sap, they found a "booby-trap," consisting of hand-grenades, attached to wire running across the trench and some trip-wire.

2. HOSTILE ATTITUDE AND ACTIVITY.

   (a) Artillery.

   Below normal on front line, unusually active against Intermediate Line.

   10.27 a.m.   21 5.9's, fired in salvos of 3, into TUMULUS VALLEY from direction N.E.

   9.0 p.m. and at intervals during night, over 200 4.2's fell in L.22.a. and c. This area was similarly shelled on night 4th/5th with 150 4.2's (not previously reported).

   LE VERGUIER was shelled with 4.2's and 7.7's during the morning.

   (b) Movement.

   9.30 a.m.   2 men working, raising parapet of trench, at G.21.c.1.7.
   9.40 a.m.   3 men, working on ST.HELENE TRENCH N.3.a.8.1., were dispersed by our artillery.
   11.10 a.m. 4 men left QUARRY WOOD and entered BANK TRENCH about G.8.c.5.5.

   ....The

The usual movement of individuals and small parties reported all along the enemy's front system throughout the day. Visibility was poor, owing to mist.

(c) Aviation.

1.30 p.m.   2 E.A. crossed the extreme right of our line, very high.
2.25 p.m.   2 E.A., high up, flew over SWAN WORK.
3.45 p.m.   1 E.A. flew over BUISSON RIDGE, high up; driven off by A.A. fire.

Bombing Attack.

4.45 a.m. - 5.45 a.m.   1 E.A., flying low, passed several times over HERVILLY and ROISEL. 9 bombs were dropped in ROISEL and several horses were killed.

3. MISCELLANEOUS.

There appears to be some shelters at H.3.b.3.9., as corrugated iron is visible there.
Chalk and earth has been thrown up along PEN TRENCH from G.33.d.3.0. to G.33.d.1.6.

4. PRESS COMMUNIQUE.

"E.A. active in early morning dropping bombs on back areas, otherwise nothing to report on Army front.
"ITALIAN front: increased artillery activity along Middle PIAVE. Our aircraft bombarded with good results hutments and aviation camps.
"RUSSIA: BOLSHEVISTS demand peace conference be transferred to neutral territory. Germany desires proceed with negotiations on German territory. Question now acute.
"German soldiers deserting in large numbers owing to being sent to Western front. 25,000 German soldiers S. of KOVNO have revolted and entrenched themselves, having rifles and M.G's. Military authorities powerless and are trying to cut off their food supplies.
"LLOYD GEORGE yesterday stated ENGLAND'S WAR AIMS:
    BELGIUM - complete restoration of independence and reparation for devastation.
    FRANCE - Restoration of ALSACE-LORRAINE.
    RUSSIA - An independent POLAND necessity for stability of Western Europe.
    CONSTANTINOPLE and DARDANELLES internationalized and neutralized.
    ITALY   - Settlement of Italian claim to union with ROUMANIA."

Captain,
G.S., Dismounted Divisions.

6th January, 1918.

CONFIDENTIAL.

SUMMARY OF INTELLIGENCE, No. 17.

H.Q. DISMOUNTED DIVISIONS.

for 24 hours ending 6 a.m. 7/1/18.

1. OPERATIONS.

   (a) Our Patrols.

   A patrol of 1 N.C.O. and 8 men left No. 8 Post at 7 p.m. and moved round E. side of ASCENSION WOOD. On reaching a point about G.26.a.1.3., a strong enemy patrol was observed about G.26.a.5.5. Our patrol retired to sunk road (G.26.a.0.0.) and the enemy advanced to N. side of ASCENSION WOOD. Our patrol then moved up sunk road to about G.25.b.5.2. and opened fire on the enemy patrol, who had moved round the N.W. corner of the wood, at about G.25.b.central. Shouts were heard from the enemy, who bolted through the N.W. corner of the wood. Our patrol remained in position at G.25.b.5.2. for 20 minutes and then returned to our lines. The enemy patrol was estimated to be 45 strong. They were not wearing white suits.

   An Officer's patrol went out at 3 a.m. and reconnoitred DOG'S LEG, SOMERVILLE WOOD & ANGLE BANK, reporting all clear.

2. HOSTILE ATTITUDE & ACTIVITY.

   (a) ARTILLERY.

   Hostile artillery was again more active against the LE VERGUIER - GRAND PRIEL WOOD area than against our front line.

   9 a.m. - 3 p.m. Our trench system in L.22.a. & b. intermittently shelled.
   9.30 am. & 10pm 6 4.2's fell near W. end of MARTEN LANE.
   11.45 am -
       12.30 pm.   20 4.2's fell about L.12.c.8.5.
   2.40 p.m.   3 H.E. shells fell about M.2.c.6.5.
   3.20 p.m.   12 H.E. shells fired into ASCENSION Fm. and No. 6 Post.
   4 - 4.30 p.m.   20 4.2's and 5.9's fell around the TUMULUS.
   7 p.m.   Slight shelling of PLEUMEL WOOD Area with H.E.

   (b) Movement.

   Considerable movement of individuals and small parties seen opposite our Right Sector all day. A few instances of enemy observers watching our line are included in the reports below, which may indicate a local relief in the near future :

   7.30 a.m.   Party of 20 men, fully equipped, entered SKIN TRENCH from QUARRY WOOD and were fired on by our H.R's.
   9.30 a.m.   2 men observed our lines from parapet of ROSE TRENCH (G.27.a.9.4.)
   10.15 a.m.   2 men in cloaks stood on parapet of LILY TRENCH (G.27.a.8.5.) observing our line for 2 minutes.
   10.30 a.m.   Working party seen in SKIN TRENCH (G.6.a.85.10.)
   1.10 p.m.   2 men, S.W. of LITTLE PEAR, one wearing great-coat. One man lying down and observing towards BERTH AUCOURT, through telescope or glasses.

   ...... 2 p.m.

2 p.m. Sniper, wearing white cap and cloak, seen firing from ONOTO TRENCH (G.33.b.2.0.) Fired on by our artillery.
2.45 p.m. 4 or 5 men, probably working party seen behind FARM TRENCH (G.14.c.4.8.)
3.15 p.m. Sentry in ONOTO TRENCH was seen to be relieved.
3.25 p.m. 4 men appeared from road G.20.d.8.7. and moved N. to G.20.d.8.9. Later, 2 more men went same way, carrying packs, also 2 going in opposite direction.

(c) Aviation.

In all, 20 E.A. were seen, of whom only the following are reported to have crossed our lines:-

11 a.m. 1 E.A. (8,000 ft.) flew in S. direction over VILLERET Area.
11.30 a.m. 1 E.A. (3,000 ft.) flew over BERTHAUCOURT towards MAISSEMY, until driven off by A.A. fire.
1.35 p.m. 1 E.A. (3,000 ft.) over LONE TREE POST, ASCENSION POSTS and retired East, under heavy A.A. fire.
2.10 p.m. 3 E.A. (7,000 ft.) flew S.W. towards VILLERET but were driven back by A.A. fire.

The heights are approximate estimates.

3. Hostile Defences.

Our Right Sector report new work in progress behind PEN TRENCH about M.3.b.8.7. Enemy working party was dispersed by French M.G's.

A newly-dug trench is also reported to run S.E. for a few yards from G.35.c.6.9.

There is a foot-bridge over the C.T. leading into WAT TRENCH at G.27.d.0.5.

W. Browne
Captain,
7th. January, 1918.   G.S., Dismounted Divisions.

C O R R I G E N D U M.
==*=*=*=*=*=*=*=*=*=*

Summary 16 of 6th. inst.

Para 1 (v). It is regretted that the patrol report was misunderstood. This sub-para should read as follows:

" The L.P. on S.E. corner of LITTLE BILL has NOT been used since last snowfall. Our patrol proposed a booby-trap, which was left there in case the enemy should return."

Appendix 1

CONFIDENTIAL.

SUMMARY OF INTELLIGENCE, No. 18.
H.Q., DISMOUNTED DIVISIONS.
for 24 hours ending 6 a.m. 8/1/18.

1. **OPERATIONS.**

   (a) **Our Patrols.**

   A patrol of 3 officers and 29 O.R. left our line at 6 p.m. and moved right round ASCENSION WOOD. They found a German cap at G.25.a.6.3. This provides no identification. The patrol then moved to G.26.a.5.7., where they remained for 20 minutes, with scouts forward in the S. portion of BIG BILL. They returned via G.20.c.5.0. and G.19.c.7.4., remaining 25 minutes at the latter point. No enemy was seen or heard. The scene of the previous night's patrol encounter was searched but only a cap was found.

   The patrol report no sign of enemy work in the S. portion of BIG BILL.

   A patrol of 2 Officers and 18 O.R. went out at 4 a.m. and reconnoitred ANGLE BANK, SOMERVILLE WOOD, and DOG'S LEG, all of which were reported clear of the enemy. The patrol returned at 5.30 a.m.

   (b) **Our M.G's and T.M's.**

   Between 6 p.m. and 9 p.m, our M.G's fired 4,000 rounds harassing fire on the following targets : QUARRY in G.14.central, BUISSON Fm. and the TRENCH TRIANGLE (G.20.a.7.9.)

   Our T.M's fired 116 rounds during the 24 hours on BANK TRENCH, SKIN TRENCH and QUARRY (G.14.a.8.8.). An enemy working-party was dispersed and 2 M.G's silenced.

2. **Hostile Attitude and Activity.**

   (a) **Artillery.**

   Again very quiet against our front line.

   9.5 a.m.   4 5.9's fell round TUMULUS.
   1.10 p.m.   Slight shelling of GRAND PRIEL Fm. and L.28. with 7.7's and 4.2's.

   The following localities were lightly shelled with 4.2's during the Day:-
   GRAND PRIEL Chateau and WOOD, HESBECOURT, HARGICOURT and FERVAQUE FARM.

   (b) **Movement.**

   Except for 2 hours in the afternoon, a thick mist prevented observation :-

2.50 p.m.	2 men working on parapet about G.27.a.8.8. They jumped into trench 3 minutes later, as light improved.
2.50 p.m.	2 men got out of LILY TRENCH to examine enemy wire, G.27.c.1.2.
3.30 p.m.	4 men looking over parapet at G.20.b.1.2.
4.2 p.m.	Smoke issuing from G.27.b.1.0.
3 - 4.30 p.m.	2 men, apparently sentries, looking over parapet, G.27.a.8.8.

   (c) **Aviation.**

   NIL.

8/1/1918.

Captain,
G.S., Dismounted Divisions.

P.T.O.

MORNING COMMUNIQUE. - 8th.

British Front, nothing to report.

Great Artillery activity on ITALIAN front.

G.O.C. at ADEN reports that on the 5th. January, a strong reconnaissance was made towards HATUM and JABIR, the defences of the former being destroyed by our troops : aeroplanes co-operated with our artillery who did great execution on the enemy's infantry in the open, with direct observation at effective range.

The KING has appointed Lord READING His High Commissioner in UNITED STATES in place of Sir CECIL SPRING RICE, H.M. Ambassador at WASHINGTON.

No service flying possible yesterday.

==*=*=*=*=*=*=*=*=*=*=*=*=*=*=*

Appendix 1

CONFIDENTIAL.

SUMMARY OF INTELLIGENCE, NO. 10.

H.Q., DISMOUNTED DIVISIONS.

for 24 hours ending 6 a.m. 9/1/18.

1. OPERATIONS.

   (a) A patrol of 3 Officers and 29 O.R. left No. 2 PRIEL Fm. POST at 12 midnight and carried out a thorough reconnaissance of BIG and LITTLE BILL. Both were found to be clear of enemy and no signs of enemy work were seen. The patrol moved round the N.E. corner of BIG BILL and round the S. side of ASCENSION WOOD, and returned to our line at 2.45 a.m.
   No tracks of any sort were found in NO MAN'S LAND.
   ANGLE BANK and SOMERVILLE WOOD were, also, reconnoitred without incident.

   (b) Our M.G's & T.M's.

   At 8.30a.m., our T.M's engaged and silenced an enemy sniper, who was firing from G.8.c.15.15.
   From 7 p.m. to midnight our T.M's also fired 100 rounds, in retaliation for enemy's aerial torpedoes, at the following targets, silencing the enemy's fire :-
   BANK TRENCH G.7.b.95.35 - G.7.b.95.45.; SKIN TRENCH G.8.a.5.5.; O.P., G.8.a.50.65.

2. Hostile Attitude and Activity.

   (a) Artillery.

   Hostile artillery was again very inactive against our front line positions. Our Centre Sector report slight shelling of back areas.

   9.45 a.m.   25 - 30 H.E. (7.7's & 4.2's) fell round ASCENSION FARM and No. 6 POST.
   11 a.m.   A few more rounds fired into same area.

   VADENCOURT and PONTRU were intermittently shelled with 5.9's during the morning.

   (b) Movement.

   7.32 a.m.   3 men came from behind SQUARE COPSE and moved off E.
   7.45 a.m.   5 men walked in open from G.20.b.8.2. towards BUISSON GAULAINE Fm.
   8.35 a.m.   3 men got out of trench at G.20.d.9.4. and stood for 3 minutes, observing our line.
   10.15 a.m.   4 men seen in enemy's wire, G.33.d.1.7.
   10.15 a.m.   5 men walked down C.T. from G.27.b.3.1. carrying what appeared to be camp-kettles.
   12 p.m.   Working party, with duck-boards, seen in BANK TRENCH, G.8.a.05.10.
   1.30 p.m.   Working party in SKIN TRENCH (G.8.a.8.1.) dispersed by our M.G's.
   4 p.m.   12 men left PEARS TRENCH at G.20.b.8.0. and walked in single file along parapet in Northerly direction, disappearing over the ridge.

   In addition to the above, the usual movement was observed along the enemy's front system, in the intervals between the snow-storms.

(c) Aviation.

E.A. very inactive.
8 a.m. 2 E.A. (3,500 ft) circled over TUMULUS for 15 minutes, and withdrew under A.A. fire.

3. Enemy Defences.

(a) Work & New Wire.

(i) New earth noticed on parapets of existing trenches at following places:
M.4.a.3.6. - G.20.d.8.5.

(ii) Small working parties seen during the day at G.20.b.2.2. - G.20.b.1.3. - G.33.d.7.4.

Both the above reports probably indicate ordinary maintenance work.

4. Miscellaneous.

(i) 11 p.m. - 11.30 p.m. the enemy fired 8 rifle grenades at our working party at G.7.b.7.6. All fell short of our trench.

(ii) There is a green camouflage screen at the junction of ROPE LANE & BANK TRENCH (G.7.b.9.6.). Men often seen passing this point.

(iii) An engine, thought to be pumping water, was plainly heard during the night, in SKIN TRENCH.

(iv) Smoke seen issuing from G.20.b.3.2. at 8 a.m., probably cooking.

                                                                       Captain,
9th. January, 1918.   G.S., Dismounted Divisions.

Evening Communique, 8th.

On night 7th/8th. 350 5.9's fired into TEMPLEUX LE GUERARD.
At 7 a.m. 8th., enemy attacked E. of BULLECOURT and gained footing in front line, but subsequently ejected by counter-attack. 18 prisoners left in our hands.
British Destroyer sunk in Mediterranean, 10 lives lost.
During, December, French accounted for 76 E.A., having lost 26 aeroplanes themselves in same period.

Morning Communique, 9th.

In WOEUVRE, big French raid successful, on front of 1500 metres. 150 prisoners and several M.G's and T.M's captured.
From April 9th. to conclusion FLANDERS Offensive and exclusive of CAMBRAI battle, following captures made :-

        57,696 prisoners (including 1,290 Officers.)
          393 guns (including 109 heavy guns.)
          561 Trench Mortars.
         1976 Machine Guns.

Appendix 1

CONFIDENTIAL.

SUMMARY OF INTELLIGENCE, NO. 20.

H.Q., DISMOUNTED DIVISIONS.

for 24 hours ending 6 a.m. 10/1/18.

1. OPERATIONS.

(a) Our Patrols.

A patrol of 3 Officers and 40 O.R. went out at 5 p.m. and reconnoitred SOMERVILLE WOOD and DOG'S LEG. They then took up a position at G.32.d.8.2., while 1 Officer and 3 O.R. advanced along the bank leading from G.33.c.0.0. to ELEVEN TREES. This officer followed the bank to within 200 yards of the TREES and then moved N. along the whole front of the ELEVEN TREES, returning to the bank at about G.33.c.6.4. They then worked back to the main body and the patrol returned to LONE TREE POST at 9 p.m.

The result of the reconnaissance of ELEVEN TREES is as follows:-

(i) No sign of recent occupation by the enemy.
(ii) 2 unused dug-outs in bank, about G.33.c.3.2. and G.33.c.6.4.
(iii) Patrol report no wire along top of bank.

The patrol reports several Very lights fired from about FILLER WORK; these fell 30 yards E. of ELEVEN TREES. Occasional bursts of M.G. fire from about M.3.a.5.3.

The ground in front of PRIEL FARM POSTS, (through G.19.b.central and d.central) was patrolled for two hours. No enemy movement seen or heard.

(b) Our M.G's and T.M's.

Our M.G's fired 6,000 rounds harassing fire between 5.30 p.m. and 9.30 p.m. on the following targets:-
Road G.14.a.55.00.
Track junction in G.14.c.
Sunk road on SENTINEL RIDGE.
BREW LANE - G.14.d.

Our T.M's fired 5 rounds at 2.30 a.m. at enemy M.G., reported active from G.7.b.90.75.

The M.G. was silenced.

2. Hostile Attitude and Activity.

(a) Artillery.

The enemy again left our front line very quiet and turned his attention to the following localities, which were shelled at intervals.
TEMPLEUX-le-GUERARD, FERVAQUE FARM, PIEUHEL WOOD, LE VERGUIER and COOKER'S QUARRY (R.11.c.8.8.)

(b) Movement.

Our Right Sector observed a great amount of movement throughout the day in the enemy's forward area, over 200 Germans being seen by their observers during daylight. Almost all this movement appears normal.
2.20 - 2.30 p.m. 3 carrying parties of 7; 2 and 4 men respectively, moving at 5 minutes intervals, left the trench at G.20.b.7.7. and walked across the open to road at G.21.a.3.0.

.... 2.30 pm

2.30 p.m.   Armed party of 45 men paraded at a house about
             G.34.b.25.15 and marched up CHOPPER RAVINE and, then
             turning off W., disappeared behind SQUARE COPSE.

3 p.m.   10 men, seen coming in W. direction from G.35.c.7.2.,
             engaged by our sniping gun. Shells burst among party
             and at least 2 were killed; party took refuge in trench
             and stretcher-bearers soon arriving.

 (c) Aviation.

10.25 a.m.   1 E.A. (2,000 ft) over ASCENSION Fm., retired S.E. under
             A.A. fire.
10.45 a.m.   1 E.A. (4,000 ft) over Centre Sector, fired at by M.G's
11.15 a.m.   1 E.A. (3,500 ft) over PONTRU.
12 noon.   2 E.A. (2,500 ft) from NAUROY flew over TUMULUS, PONTRU
             and VADENCOURT, until driven off by A.A. fire.
12.30 p.m.   1 E.A. (1,000 ft) over ASCENSION VALLEY - did not cross our
             lines.
12.30 p.m.   2 E.A. (5,000 ft) over Centre Sector fired at by M.G's.
12.10 - 1.10 1 E.A. (6pp ft) patrolled over SQUARE COPSE, crossed our
   p.m.   lines over DRAGOON POST but retired under our fire.

3. Hostile Defences.

 (a) Work and new trenches.

 Working parties reported at following places:-
  (i) G.20.b.9.2., behind existing trench. 7 men working all
   morning.
  (ii) G.20.b.7.3., party working with timber.
 (iii) About G.28.c.50.25 - 9 men digging.

 (b) Wire.

 Gap reported in wire at M.3.c.9.5.
 See also patrol report in para 1 re wire along bank in G.33.c.

 (c) M.G's and T.M's.

 M.G. emplacement reported in SWAN WORK.
 2 men also seen with M.G. at G.20.d.8.7.

4. Hostile Organization.

 (a) Dumps.
 Dump reported at G.34.d.7.7., where a black and white flag can
 be seen. Carrying party of 12 - 15 men seen working there at
 2 p.m.

 (b) Communications.

 3 men reported working on telephone wires at G.21.a.8.6.

5. Miscellaneous.

 (i) At 11 a.m., 1 man was observed climbing down the right hand tree
of RUBY WOOD (viewed from the S.E.) - probably an O.P.
 (ii) An enemy battery carried out the following shoot from 3 - 3.30
p.m. yesterday :-
  2 shells burst 20 yds. N. of VICTORIA X roads.
  2   "   "   20 " S.   "   "   "
  2   "   "   over ONOTO TRENCH.
 All six gave off yellow smoke.
 Then 8 shells burst in ASCENSION VALLEY, giving off black smoke.
It appears probable, that a new battery had come in and was registering it's S.O.S. barrage.

                    Captain,
10th. January, 1918. G.S., Dismounted Divisions.

Appendix 1

CONFIDENTIAL.

SUMMARY OF INTELLIGENCE, NO. 21.

H.Q. DISMOUNTED DIVISIONS.

for 24 hours ending 6 a.m. 11/1/18.

1. OPERATIONS.

   (a) Our patrols.

   A patrol of 2 Officers and 30 O.R. left our lines at 5.30 p.m. and moved round W. and N. edges of ASCENSION WOOD to G.25.b.9.6., where they lay in ambush for 2 hours, with scouts in the valley to the N. and N.E. No enemy patrol was seen or heard and patrol returned round the N. point of ASCENSION WOOD and reached our line at 9 p.m.
   DOG'S LEG, ANGLE BANK and SOMERVILLE WOOD were reconnoitred and reported clear of the enemy.
   A patrol of 1 N.C.O. and 2 men reconnoitred the enemy's wire in G.7.b. They report enemy's wire good; no gaps were found; 2 men heard moving in BANK TRENCH about G.8.a.0.3. and a M.G. was seen firing from G.8.a.1.2.
   A patrol of 1 Officer and 4 O.R. reconnoitred the bank in L.18.c. and G.13.d. This patrol report no signs of enemy work on this bank, but they found two strong trip-wires along the bank.

   (b) Our M.G's and T.M's.

   Our M.G's fired 4,000 rounds harassing fire on to targets around LA HAUTE BRUYERE, between 5.30 p.m. and 6.40 p.m.
   Our T.M's fired 61 rounds during the 24 hours on to the following targets:-
   Enemy working party G.8.c.20.85;
   QUARRY G.14.a.8.7.; railway G.8.c.5.5.; trench G.8.c.2.4.

2. Hostile Attitude and Activity.

   (a) Artillery.

   Enemy's artillery was again active against the HARGICOURT - LE VERGUIER Line.
   Our Right Sector report PONTRU Area shelled with 5.9's at 8 a.m. and 2.20 p.m. - otherwise very little shelling of the forward area.
   The following localities were shelled at intervals during the day with 4.2's and 5.9's : LE VERGUIER (40 4.2's between 9 a.m. and 11 a.m.); L.16.d.; FERVAQUE FM.; L.15.b.; HARGICOURT ; L.3.; TEMPLEUX le GUERARD.

   (b) Movement.

   Abnormal movement reported in BELLENGLISE area and between NAUROY and ETRICOURT, but mostly movement of individuals and small groups.
   Several of the parties seen reported to have been carrying bundles. This tends to confirm the suspected Divisional relief.

8.0 a.m.	84 men standing on road G.34.b.8.7. Another large party arrived. Our artillery informed.
10.25 a.m.	Armed party of about 30 men, in open order, moving from about G.27.d.0.5. towards BELL COPSE.
11.0 a.m.	4 men leave ST. HELENE TRENCH and disappear over Ridge in N.N.E. direction - later seen going into house at G.34.b.25.15. Followed at 15 minutes intervals by 2 parties of 5 and 3. This is of particular interest as

......ST. HELENE

-2-

ST. HELENE TRENCH appeared unoccupied during the snow.

- 12.0 noon. Group of about 30 men standing outside house at G.34.b.25.15. They move off N.W. up CHOPPER RAVINE.
- 2.45 p.m. 3 men walking in open about G.33.d.8.8., one of whom points out objects all the time.
- 4.0 p.m. 20 men in road G.35.c.20.75.
- " " 14 men walking about G.35.d.7.8.

(c) Aviation.

E.A. very inactive.

1.0 p.m. 2 E.A. flying low towards VILLERET, were driven off by our aeroplanes before crossing our line.

3. HOSTILE DEFENCES.

(a) Work and New Trenches.

The usual number of small working parties was seen, but several of these were specially reported to be carrying timber and planks into the front trenches (notably WAT TRENCH and BANK TRENCH). This was, also, a feature of yesterday's reports and applies to the whole of the enemy's front system. It is thought that the enemy may be busy constructing new dugouts.

Working parties were reported digging at the following points:-
G.20.b.4.5., G.29.d.9.2.(party there all day), G.20.b.7.3.(1½hours).

(b) Communications.

Men seen repairing air-line at W. edge of BILLIARD COPSE.

4. HOSTILE ORGANISATION.   G.31.d.7.7.

The Dump, reported in yesterday's Summary, at
was again the scene of continual activity during the day.

[signature] Captain,

G.S., Dismounted Divisions.

11th January, 1918.

Appendix 1

CONFIDENTIAL.

SUMMARY OF INTELLIGENCE, No. 22.

H.Q., DISMOUNTED DIVISIONS.

for 24 hours ending 8.0 a.m. 12/1/18.

1. OPERATIONS.

   Our Patrols.

   A patrol of 3 Officers and 30 O.R. left our line at 5.30 p.m. and moved to the N. side of LITTLE BILL, remaining there while scouts reconnoitred the Copse. They then proceeded to the N.E. corner of BIG BILL, which their scouts reported all clear. The patrol waited here in ambush for 30 minutes, but no sign of enemy movement was seen. They then moved to about G.25.b.8.8., remaining there for half an hour, and regained our line at 9.15 p.m.

   ANGLE BANK, SOMERVILLE WOOD and DOG'S LEG were reconnoitred as usual and reported clear of enemy.

2. HOSTILE ATTITUDE AND ACTIVITY.

   (a) Artillery.

   Increased activity reported, except against front line system, where shelling was reported normal.

   7.20 a.m.   5 4.2's fell in VILLERET.
   9.30 - 10.30 a.m.   20 4.2's fell in VADENCOURT.
   9.23 a.m.   3 4.2's behind DRAGOON POST.
   3.30 - 7.30 p.m.   The areas L.15, L.16, L.21 and L.22 were heavily shelled with over 200 4.2's and 5.9's.

   The following localities were shelled during the day:-

   LE VERGUIER (90 4.2's and 5.9's).
   L.28.b. and L.23.a.

   (b) Movement.

   7.30 a.m.   Party of about 8 men standing outside house G.34.b.25.15. Continual movement again reported to and from this house.
   8.0 a.m.   2 men, apparently officers, left trench G.20.b.5.2. and disappeared in E. direction, followed 3 minutes later by 3 men, carrying packs.
   10.0 a.m.   Large party, who had been working at G.24.a.4.9., dispersed by our guns.
   10.30 a.m.   Stretcher-bearers reported moving to same place.

   Visibility was poor in the morning and very bad later, but our Right Sector reported the usual movement of small parties, especially in and around BELLENGLISE.
   PEARL TRENCH and WAT TRENCH appear to have been flooded, as enemy was seen baling.

3. HOSTILE DEFENCES.

   A working party of 10 or more men was seen at G.29.d.9.2. from 8.45 a.m. until 10.15 a.m., when they went away, leaving their tools.

12th January, 1918.

Captain,
G.S., Dismounted Divisions.

CONFIDENTIAL.

SUMMARY OF INTELLIGENCE, No. 23.

H.Q., DISMOUNTED DIVISIONS.

for 24 hours ending 6.0 a.m. 13/1/18.

1. OPERATIONS.

(a) Our Patrols.

A patrol of 2 Officers and 33 O.R., who left our line at 5.30 p.m., went to FISHER CRATER and on towards ST. HELENE TRENCH, where voices were heard. But snow had started to fall since the patrol started, and, as they were not in white suits, they could not approach the enemy's wire.

A patrol of 2 Officers and 30 other ranks left our line at 8.0 p.m. and reconnoitred BUISSON RIDGE. They went to about L.13.d.4.4. and then moved S. to about G.19.b.6.6., where they remained for half an hour. Scouts reconnoitred the bushes at G.14.c.0.0. The front and flanks of the bushes had several lines of low wire running round them, about 50 yards from the bushes. But owing to the extent of the wire and the lack of previous information about it, further action seemed inadvisable. The patrol returned at 11.0 p.m.

An Officer's patrol went out from RAILWAY TRENCH and made a thorough reconnaissance of the enemy's wire.

(b) Our M.G's and T.M's.

Between 5.45 and 7.0 p.m., our M.G's fired 4,000 rounds harassing fire at the following targets:-

BREW LANE, G.14.d.
Sunk road, G.8.a.
SENTINEL RIDGE.

Our T.M's fired 115 rounds during the night in retaliation on the following targets:-

Suspected T.M's, G.14.a.8.7., G.14.a.6.8. and G.8.c.30.85.
Dug-outs G.8.a.8.0.
Camouflage screen G.8.a.35.50.
M.G's firing from G.8.a.1.3., G.7.b.9.7. - both were silenced.

2. HOSTILE ATTITUDE AND ACTIVITY.

(a) Artillery.

The enemy's activity against our Centre Sector is on the increase.

9.0 - 10 a.m.	12 4.2's in ASCENSION FARM and G.25.c.central.
12.45 - 1.30 p.m.	50 4.2's fell near ONION LANE and railway at L.11.b.9.8.
12.45 - 1.20 p.m.	7 4.2's, instantaneous bursts, S.E. of COTE WOOD, 4 more at 3.45 p.m.
1.45 - 3.0 p.m.	LE VERGUIER, ASCENSION and GRAND PRIEL FM's shelled at 5 minute intervals by 4.2's and 5.9's under aeroplane observation.
3.30 p.m.	12 4.2's about G.31.d.8.2.
4.55 - 5.15 p.m.	30 4.2's and 7.7's fell around L.10.c.5.5.
5.30 - 7.20 p.m.	200 4.2's and 5.9's fired into area around COTE WOOD.

TUMULUS and VADENCOURT slightly shelled during the day.

...(b)

(b) Movement.

8.10 a.m.   Party of 15 men move from G.21.c.5.4. into trench at G.21.c.5.1.
12.15 p.m. 2-horsed limbered wagon seen on road (G.34.c.) - big white disc on back of limber.
12.15 p.m. Small parties of the enemy, who gathered round our fallen aeroplane in G.28.a., were engaged with good effect by our artillery.

The usual movement of individuals was seen in BANK TRENCH, and continual movement of individuals and small parties reported opposite our Right Sector.

Continual movement was again reported at the house about G.34.b.25.15. Normal traffic was seen on the road G.35.b.1.4.

The enemy was seen baling water out of BANK, SKIN and WAT TRENCHES.

(c) Aviation.

See Late News below.

3. HOSTILE DEFENCES.

(a) Work & New Trenches.

Working parties were seen at the following points:-
G.23.b.1.4. (5 men for 30 minutes); G.29.d.9.2. - men keep on carrying timber to this party. See also Summary No.22, para. 3; G.24.a.30.95.(7 men); G.27.a.9.4.; G.2.c.1.9.; PIPE TRENCH (G.14.a.35.50).

New work appears to be in progress in G.20.b., just S.E. of BUISSON GAULAINE FM., where small working parties were reported digging a trench.

Alteration to SWAN WORK was noticed: the large chalk mound in the parapet has been levelled down.

(b) Wire.

At 9.35 a.m. 10 men were reported repairing wire at G.3.a.2.5. New wiring reported at G.34.c.8.8..

4. MISCELLANEOUS.

(i) At 12 noon, a flag or board, halved red and white, was seen on parapet of BANK TRENCH G.2.c.10.45. A similar occurrence was reported at RUBY WOOD on 9th instant.

(ii) A small metal cylinder was picked up from a new shell-hole near COTE WOOD. This was handed over for expert examination.

(iii) A gun was seen firing from S. edge of ETRICOURT at 10.25 a.m. (G.18.d.9.1.)

(iv) At 5.0 p.m. a light was observed flashing from the direction of MAGNY-LA-FOSSE, apparently a man signalling with a torch. Only the latter part of the message was read, which ran as follows:-
"......there, otherwise new work cannot progress here. It is dark and there is no light and nothing can be done. Good night. Sleep well."

(v) Abnormal movement in back area reported last 3 days has now ceased.

5. LATE NEWS - Aviation.

12.0 - 1.0 p.m. 2 E.A. flew low along RAILWAY TRENCH, patrolling to and fro.

Captain,
G.S., Dismounted Divisions.

13th January, 1917.

Appendix 1

CONFIDENTIAL.   SUMMARY OF INTELLIGENCE, No. 24.

H.Q., DISMOUNTED DIVISIONS.

for 24 hours ending 6.0 a.m. 14/1/18.

1. OPERATIONS.

   (a) Our Patrols.

   2 Patrols reconnoitred the enemy's wire opposite RAILWAY TRENCH and accomplished their mission without incident.

   A Patrol also reconnoitred NO MAN'S LAND in G.19.d. at 3.30 a.m. without finding any trace of the enemy.

   NOTE: In para. 1 of yesterday's Summary (No.23), the following point was omitted from the account of the reconnaissance of BUISSON RIDGE:-

   "An enemy sentry-post (2 men) was seen at the S.W. edge of the bushes."

   See also "Special Report", para. 2 (b), below.

   (b) Our M.G's and T.M's.

   Our T.M's dispersed an enemy working-party at midnight at G.8.a.5.6., and at 2 a.m. they silenced an enemy M.G. about G.8.c.25.75. 20 rounds retaliation fire were fired at O.T. in G.14.a.7.6. and at BANK TRENCH, G.7.b.90.65.

2. HOSTILE ATTITUDE AND ACTIVITY.

   (a) Artillery.

   The enemy's artillery again showed marked activity against our Centre Sector.

10.30 - 11.15 a.m.	20 5.9's fell about L.10.a.2.2.
" " "	4 salvoes from 4 field guns burst 50 yards beyond COTE TRENCH in L.10.d.
12.15 p.m.	15 H.E. shells fired into SOMERVILLE WOOD.
2.20 - 2.30 p.m.	20 5.9's fell in L.16.central.
2.30 - 3.0 p.m.	MARTEN LANE shelled with 4.2's
3.0 - 3.30 p.m.	50 5.9's fell about L.9.d.central.
3.30 p.m.	6 salvoes of 4 field guns (shrapnel) and 6 5.9's burst about G.10.b.4.0.
3.40 p.m.	17 5.9's fell around ASCENSION FARM and No.6 Post.
5.30 p.m. & 7.30 p.m.	25 H.E. shells burst round S.2 Post.
7.0 - 7.40 p.m.	Area L.10.d. and L.16.b. shelled with H.E.

   LE VERGUIER also shelled at 45 minutes intervals throughout the day. An aeroplane was reported observing for this shoot at 8.45 a.m.

   (b) Movement.

   Normal movement was seen all along the enemy's front line system. Small parties were observed in BANK and SKIN TRENCHES, evidently engaged on draining and repairing the trenches.

11.0 a.m.	4 men stood on parapet for a few minutes at G.27.a.5.8.
11.30 a.m.	5 men stood on top of trench at G.20.d.8.6.
1.45 p.m.	1 mounted man going S. down road in G.34.a.
3.30 p.m.	1 Wagon (2 horses) " " " " " "

   ....SPECIAL

Special Report.

Observers were posted at L.24.a.7.0. before dawn on morning of 13th to report on movement in bushes at G.14.c.0.0., where a double sentry-post was reported by patrol on night 12/13th.

At 7 a.m. a party of 10 men left the bushes, crossed road by small trench at G.14.c.2.1., making towards G.14.c.7.0., but could not be seen actually entering trench. A M.G., G.14.c.5.1., was seen. N.N.W. of bushes 2 rows, of 5 thick poles, each about 6 ft. high and beyond them a short piece of trench. No wire could be seen.

(c) Aviation.

Several E.A. seen but only 4 crossed our line.

9.0 a.m. 1 E.A. (3,000 ft.) flew from NAUROY direction over DRAGOON POST and BERTHAUCOURT and then made off E. under A.A. fire.
1.15 p.m. 3 E.A. (4,000 ft.) flew over FARM SUPPORT but retired S.E. under A.A. fire.

3. HOSTILE DEFENCES.

Work and New Trenches.

Enemy working party of 18 men seen at BIG BEAR at 2.0 p.m.

4. MISCELLANEOUS.

An observer made a parachute descent at 2.30 p.m. from an enemy balloon, which was up just behind ETRICOURT. The man landed S.W. of MAGNY-LA-FOSSE — apparently a practice descent, as the balloon remained up until 3.30 p.m.

14th January, 1918.

Captain,
G.S., Dismounted Divisions.

Appendix 1

CONFIDENTIAL.   SUMMARY OF INTELLIGENCE, No. 25.

H.Q., DISMOUNTED DIVISIONS.

for 24 hours ending 6.0 a.m. 15/1/18.
==*=*=*=*=*=*=*=*=*=*=*=*=*=*=*=*=*=*

1. OPERATIONS.

   (a) Our Patrols.

   A patrol of 3 Officers and 80 O.R. carried out a valuable reconnaissance of ST. HELENE TRENCH.
   The patrol left our line at 6.0 p.m. and moved to FISHER CRATER, where they put out a strong covering party N. of the Crater. They then divided into 2 parties which acted as follows:-

   Northern Party cut enemy's wire and entered ST. HELENE TRENCH at M.3.a.8.1., where it is in very bad repair and is obviously disused. As the frozen state of the ground made quiet movement almost impossible, the patrol leader went on from this point with only 2 men and reconnoitred in a N.E. direction.
   He reported as follows:-
   (i) The enemy's wire in front of the trench, which runs from M.3.b.4.9. to M.3.a.85.75., is very strong and could not be cut by hand.

   (ii) Enemy M.G. was firing short bursts from M.3.d.1.7.
   (iii) Very Lights were being fired frequently from PEN TRENCH.
   (iv) Digging and movement was heard in the trench (about M.3.b.0.7).
   (v) Enemy working party was also heard further E.

   The patrol leader, finding this trench held and strongly wired, rejoined his patrol at M.3.a.8.1.

   Southern Patrol cut the enemy's wire and entered ST. HELENE TRENCH at M.3.d.10.65. They moved E. along this trench for 300 yards and found no sign of any enemy. The patrol leader, with 6 men, then reconnoitred the ground between the trench and the BELLENGLISE Road at M.3.b.2.8. This ground and the BELLENGLISE Road were both clear of the enemy.
   This Southern patrol then moved round to the North and joined the other party. They made another gap in the wire at M.3.a.85.25.
   The whole patrol then moved back to our line, reconnoitring the following localities en route:-
   FISHER CRATER, MAX WOOD, DOG'S LEG and ELEVEN TREES.

   (b) Our M.G's and T.M's.

   Our M.G's fired 4,000 rounds harassing fire during the night at the Quarry (G.14. central) and DIAMOND COPSE (G.8.b.).

2. HOSTILE ATTITUDE AND ACTIVITY.

   (a) Artillery.

   Enemy's artillery again very active against Centre Sector.

8.30 - 11.0 a.m.	60 5.9's and 4.2's fell near L.9.d.9.9.
9.15 a.m.	11 shells fell in SOMERVILLE WOOD.
11.30 a.m.	6 4.2's fell in MAXIM LANE.
12.45 - 1.30 p.m.	Over 150 5.9's and 4.2's fell near L.9.d.9.9.
1.40 - 3.15 p.m.	30 5.9's in same area.
8.0 - 8.15 p.m.	140 4.2's fell around VILLERET LANE.
8.0 - 8.20 p.m.	L.23.b. shelled with 4.2's. 2 direct hits on HARRODS STORES but no damage done.

   ......The

The following area was shelled intermittently throughout the 24 hours with 5.9's and 4.2's:-
L.10.c., L.10.d., L.16 and L.22.
LE VERGUIER was shelled at intervals during the day, and VADENCOURT was slightly shelled at mid-day.

(b) Movement.

The usual movement was seen all day along the enemy's front system, also in, and N. of, BELLENGLISE. Movement is continually seen on track from PINK TRENCH into CHOPPER RAVINE and BELLENGLISE.

7.55 a.m.   17 men cut across the open from C.T. into PINK TRENCH at G.27.a.9.7.
8.10 a.m.   4 men left the post at G.27.d.8.9.
8.50 a.m.   2 men lifted, what appeared to be a M.G., off parapet at G.8.c.3.7.
9.0 - 9.30 a.m.   2 men observing our line from G.8.c.5.4.

Small parties seen at G.34.d.9.8. all day.

(c) Aviation.

Nil.

3. HOSTILE DEFENCES.

Work was seen to be in progress at the following points:-

G.21.c.5.4.; In SKIN TRENCH (G.8.a.85.10); G.2.b.4.5.; G.2.b.1.4.;

4. MISCELLANEOUS.

At G.27.b.0.½ there are signs of new earthworks, apparently tops of new shelters, as smoke can be seen issuing from them.
On the wire in front, there are 2 small white boards probably to show the way through the wire at night.

W.P.BROWNE,
Captain, G.S.,
15th January, 1918.   G.S., Dismounted Divisions.

Appendix 1

CONFIDENTIAL.   SUMMARY OF INTELLIGENCE, No. 26.
H.Q., DISMOUNTED DIVISIONS.
for 24 hours ending 6.0 a.m. 16/1/18.

1. **OPERATIONS.**

   (a) *Our Patrols.*

   Only the usual protective patrols went out.

   (b) *Enemy Raids.*

   The enemy made a silent raid on one of our small posts at M.8.b.7.1., as a result of which 2 of our men are reported missing. No details have been received.

   (c) *Our M.G's and T.M's.*

   At 10.0 p.m., our T.M's fired 40 rounds at an enemy M.G. at G.8.a.70.10, which was silenced. Our T.M's also fired 65 rounds retaliation against BANK and SKIN TRENCHES.

2. **HOSTILE ATTITUDE AND ACTIVITY.**

   (a) *Artillery.*

   Enemy's activity against our Centre Sector continues.
   1.45 p.m.   5 7.7's burst over ELEVEN TREES - probably gun registering S.O.S. barrage.
   3.10 - 3.25 p.m. RAILWAY TRENCH and SUPPORT TRENCH shelled with 7.7's.
   3.40 p.m.   "   "   "   shelled by small T.M.
   The following localities were shelled during the late afternoon and evening with upwards of 300 shells:- COTE WOOD and TRENCH, FERVAQUE FM. and JEANCOURT - HARGICOURT Road.

   (b) *Movement.*

   The usual movement of individuals and small parties was seen along the whole of the enemy's front system opposite us.
   8.15 a.m.   5 men carrying food containers from G.14.central to G.14.c.6.8.
   9.15 a.m.   2 men, believed to be Officers, seen at G.8.c.5.5., observing our line in G.7.d. with glasses They appeared, also, to be watching VILLERET. They wore peaked caps.
   1.0 p.m.   10 men seen carrying beams up C.T. G.20.b.7.7.
   2.45 p.m.   12 men, in two's and three's, moved over HELENE RIDGE into trench at G.33.b.2.2.

   (c) *Aviation*   No activity.

3. **HOSTILE DEFENCES.**

   (a) *Work and New Trenches.*

   At 2.45 p.m., 1 man was seen on the top of the trench at G.20.d.8.7., apparently directing work. Earth was being thrown over the parapet.
   A small working party was seen in SKIN TRENCH G.8.a.

   (b) *M.G's and T.M's.*
   At 3.45 p.m., after enemy T.M. had stopped firing (see para.2 (a) above), 3 men entered dug-out at G.8.a.1.2., carrying what was thought to be a light trench mortar.

                                                    Captain,
                                        G.S., Dismounted Divisions.
16th January.1918.

CONFIDENTIAL.   SUMMARY OF INTELLIGENCE No. 27.

H.Q., DISMOUNTED DIVISIONS.

for 24 hours ending 6.0 a.m. 17/1/18.

1. OPERATIONS.

(a) **Our Raid.**
A successful, silent raid was carried out at 2.30 a.m. this morning by 2 Officers and 40 O.R. The raid was made against RANK TRENCH, between G.8.c.3.7. and G.8.a.1.2., with the object of securing an identification.
The raiding party was divided into 2 parties. The Northern party, consisting only of 1 Officer, 1 N.C.O. and 4 O.R., entered the trench at G.8.a.1.2., where they found and captured a German sentry. They returned to our lines with their prisoner.
The Southern party were seriously hampered by the bad state of the ground. A full report has not yet been received.

(b) **Our Patrols.**
A patrol left our line at 6 a.m. and reconnoitred the following localities, all of which were clear of the enemy:- SOMERVILLE WOOD, ASCENSION VALLEY, DOG'S LEG and MAX WOOD.

(c) **Enemy Raid, night 15/16th.**
Further details of the enemy's raid on our post at M.8.b.7.1. are as follows:- the enemy surrounded our post and threw bombs. 2 of our men are missing and one men from the Division on our right was wounded but escaped. The boisterous weather was greatly in favour of the enemy and prevented the alarm being given.

2. DISTRIBUTION OF ENEMY'S FORCES.
A prisoner of 3rd Bav. Ersatz I.R. (9th Bav.Res.Div.) was captured at 2.30 a.m. this morning at G.8.a.1.2. in our successful raid. This establishes the relief of the 5th Guards Division and helps to account for the abnormal movement reported E. of BELLICOURT between Jan.10th - 12th.
For details of examination, see *para. 5* overleaf.

3. HOSTILE ATTITUDE AND ACTIVITY.

(a) **Artillery.**
Enemy's artillery was less active than during the last few days.
10.30 - 10.50 a.m.   MAXIM LANE and S. end of VILLERET shelled with 4.2's and 7.7's.
5.30 - 5.50 p.m.   15 5.9's just N. of COTE WOOD.
8.0 - 8.30 p.m.   20 4.2's in same area.
The following localities were slightly shelled:- M.1.b. and d., M.2.c., M.8.central and ASCENSION FARM.

(b) **Movement.**
The usual movement was reported along the enemy's front system and in the BELLENGLISE area. This was mainly movement of individuals:-
7.0 a.m.   23 men, with blankets and all equipment, left BANK TRENCH at G.8.a.1.3., moving towards QUARRY WOOD.
7.0 - 9.0 a.m.   Several small parties, amounting to nearly 400 men in all, were seen leaving trench at G.2.b.3.0. and moving E. along MOUNT OLYMPUS. Small parties also seen going in opposite direction. These amounted to about 180. Movement was very slow and men appeared covered in mud above their knees; they were not wearing gum boots.
7.45 a.m.   16 men left front line at various points, moving across the open, and jumped into trench at G.20.b.5.0.
10.15 a.m.   2 men got out of PINK TRENCH, G.27.b.0.7. One man appeared to be supporting the other, who was reeling about and gesticulating wildly - probably drunk.
.....11.25 a.m.

-2-

11.25 a.m.   Transport wagon seen on road G.34.c.8.8.
12.15 p.m.   25 men, reported to be a working party at G.27.b.3.7.,
              were dispersed by our artillery.

(c) Aviation.   NIL.

4. HOSTILE DEFENCES.
   (a) Work and New Trenches.
       Working party of 25 men reported at G.27.b.3.6. and G.27.b.3.7.
were dispersed by our artillery.
       Large working parties were seen with duckboards in M.2.a..
       The enemy was busy baling water out of several of his trenches.
       The trench from G.8.c.2.4. to G.8.c.3.6. appears to have fallen in
as men were seen to get out and walk along the top.

   (b) Wire.   At 3.30 p.m., 5 men were wiring in front of trench at
                                            G.21.c.5.4.for 5 minutes.

5. Examination of a Prisoner captured by our left Dismounted Division
   about G.8.a. during the night 16/17th Jan. 1918.

   1. Statements.

       Prisoner belongs to 3rd Bavarian Ersatz Infantry Regiment, 9th
   Bavarian Reserve Division. He gives the correct regiments of the
   Division but cannot state the order of Battle, except that he is
   positive that his Regiment is in the Centre and that all three are in
   line. His Regiment has 2 Battalions in line and one in Reserve. Each
   Bn. has 2 Companies in line and two in support. The actual front line,
   (BANK TRENCH) is not held at all, as it has been in a very bad state
   ever since the thaw, but there are 6 men in a dug-out in BANK TRENCH
   who keep a lookout, taking a turn one at a time, by mutual
   arrangement. No N.C.O. has been near them for days and no one takes
   any interest in them. SKIN TRENCH is probably regarded as the first
   line, held by the 2 companies of the Battalion.
       Prisoner is certain that the 5th Guard Division has gone, for he
   relieved some of them. The Prussians seem to have handed over badly,
   and they advised the Bavarians to adopt a quiet policy (IN RUHE
   LASSEN), but prisoner does not know anything about intentions.

   2. Personality.

       Prisoner is a good-natured Bavarian, and a Farm labourer by
   occupation. He is intelligent enough but takes so little interest
   in soldiering that his military value as a source of information is
   greatly diminished, in spite of his willingness to talk and his lucid
   descriptions. He possesses a sense of humour, but is easily the
   worst soldier imaginable. Asked as to what he had done with his
   rifle, he said that he   really could not remember when he had
   seen it last, but that in any case it was full of mud, like
   everything else in the trench. He was quite unarmed when taken on
   sentry, but had his gas helmet which, he said, was quite enough to
   keep in order. He was called up in 1915 and had 10 weeks training
   (UNGEDIENTER LANDSTURM). His data, as far as they can be checked,
   are correct. He had heard say that German prisoners were well
   treated by us, and he had not the slightest hesitation in saying that
   he considered himself extremely well off to be taken prisoner.

6. MISCELLANEOUS.

       Considerable noise of transport was heard last night W. of
   BELLENGLISE.

                                                    Captain, G.S.,
   17th January, 1918.   G.S., Dismounted Divisions.

CONFIDENTIAL

SUMMARY OF INTELLIGENCE No. 28.

H.Q., DISMOUNTED DIVISIONS.

For 24 hours ending 6.0 a.m. 18/1/1918.

1. OPERATIONS.

(a) Our Patrols.

Patrols visited ASCENSION WOOD, the S.W. corner of BIG BILL and the W. edge of SOMERVILLE WOOD. No signs of the enemy were seen.

(b) Enemy Patrols.

Early this morning, the Brigade on our right reported an enemy patrol moving towards our post at M.8.b.7.1. Patrols went out at once but could find no trace of the enemy.

2. HOSTILE ATTITUDE AND ACTIVITY.

(a) Artillery.

The enemy's activity against our Centre Sector has subsided, and only slight shelling of the Battery Zone is reported.

W.30 - 3.15 p.m.	25 4.2's fell on and around the TUMULUS. During this shelling, 3 puffs of white smoke were seen to rise behind FILLER WORK, at 15 minutes' interval.
3.30 - 4.15 p.m.	10 4.2's fired into S. part of PONTRU.
	20 4.2's and H.E. shrapnel burst just N. of river in R.12.c.
3.30 - 4.45 p.m.	30 4.2's fell just N. of COTE WOOD.
5.45 - 6.15 p.m.	15 4.2's fired at HARGICOURT - JEANCOURT Road.
	11 5.9's fell in TEMPLEUX-le-GUERARD.
8.5 p.m.	8 rounds from H.V. gun burst S. of BIHECOURT. The flash of the gun was observed due E. from DRAGOON POST. Time between flash of discharge and flash of burst was 21 seconds.

(b) Enemy's M.G's and T.M's.

At 4.15 p.m., a M.G. fired from about G.8.c.3.6. on RAILWAY TRENCH.
A M.G., firing into the E. end of BERTHAUCOURT, was located by flash at about M.3.c.9.9.
A M.G. fired on DRAGOON and LONE TREE Posts at intervals during the 24 hours. This gun is believed to fire from ELEVEN TREES.
Enemy T.M's fired on RAILWAY TRENCH at 4.15 p.m., from about G.8.c.5.5.

(c) Movement.

The usual movement of individuals and small parties was seen along enemy's front system, especially in G.33.d. and in BELLENGLISE. One point of special interest was that in several instances, the men seen had packs on - reported in sector ST. HELENE - BUISSON GAULAINE FM.
Visibility was bad.

9.0 a.m.	Our H.R's dispersed enemy working-party near G.14.a.3.3.
12 noon.	2 men left ELEVEN TREES and went to ONOTO TRENCH, returning with a box. At 3.15 p.m., some bright object was thrown from here. It is thought that the enemy has a M.G. post here - vide para. 2 (b) above.
	.......1.35 p.m.

1.35 p.m.   8 men seen walking between ROSE and PINK TRENCHES (at
            G.27.b.1.5.) where they remained for 12 minutes.

   Several small working-parties seen during day in BANK and SKIN
TRENCHES, baling water, carrying duck-boards and digging.

   (c) Aviation.

       N I L.

3. HOSTILE DEFENCES.

   (a) Work and New Trenches.

       12 men seen working at G.34.d.9.9. in afternoon.
       12 "   "   "   " G.27.b.2.4. from 3.15 p.m. onwards.

   (b) M.G's.

       See para. 2 (b) above.

                                                        ——————— Captain,
18th January, 1918.   G.S., Dismounted Divisions.

Appendix 1

CONFIDENTIAL.   SUMMARY OF INTELLIGENCE, No. 29.

H.Q., DISMOUNTED DIVISIONS.

For 24 hours ending 6.0 a.m., 19/1/18.

1. OPERATIONS.

   (a) Our Patrols.

   An Officer's patrol left our line at 10.0 p.m. and moved to the N.W. corner of ASCENSION WOOD and thence along W. edge of BIG BILL to LITTLE BILL. A careful search was then made for the supposed enemy L.P. in G.19.d.8.8. 2 deep shell-holes, roughly connected up, were found, but shewed no sign of recent use.
   The patrol returned to our line at 12.20 a.m., having seen no sign of the enemy, but they report being sniped at when crossing the track from LITTLE BILL to ASCENSION WOOD.

   A patrol of 1 Officer and 10 men left TURNIP LANE at 11.0 p.m. and reconnoitred towards FARM TRENCH. They passed without difficulty through 2 belts of wire about G.14.a.1.2. They report that there was one more belt between them and the enemy's trench. On approaching this belt, they saw parties of the enemy in front of the trench, moving to cut off our patrol. As our patrols were between belts of the enemy's wire and were also outnumbered, they withdrew to our line. No shots were fired.

   (b) Our M.G's and T.M's.

   Our M.G's fired 2,000 rounds harassing fire on each of the following targets from 10.0 p.m. to 11.0 p.m.:-
   ROPE LANE (G.8.b.)
   N.W. corner of DIAMOND COPSE.

2. HOSTILE ATTITUDE AND ACTIVITY.

   A slight increase of hostile activity is reported against our Right Sub-sector.

   10.50 a.m.   6 7.7's (shrapnel) burst over VILLERET.
   11.30 a.m. - 12.15 p.m. Enemy shelled ridge L.15.a.
   11.30 a.m.   4 5.9's fell at L.26.c.3.4. (JEANCOURT).
   12 noon.   15 4.2's fired into LONE TREE POST.

   (b) Movement.

   The normal movement was reported along the enemy's front system. The enemy's trenches appear to be in a very bad state. Several parties were seen baling water and repairing the parapet. Movement across the open was frequently observed, particularly from G.14.a.2.2 to G.14.a.5.6. - PIPE TRENCH being apparently flooded.

   7.0 a.m.   Small party seen to leave ELEVEN TREES, carrying what appeared to be 2 M.G's or automatic rifles.
   10.55 a.m. 10 men move along top of NIB TRENCH from G.33.b.1.5. to G.33.b.2.0.
   1.20 p.m. 12 men entered SKIN TRENCH at G.2.c.7.4., where they appeared to dump something, and returned to BELLICOURT
   8.0 p.m.   Enemy wiring party (about 15 strong) at G.8.c.3.4, surprised by our Very lights and fired on.
   Activity was noticed at SWAN WORK during the day and movement of 2 or 3 men at a time was frequently observed between G.33.b.1.8. and G.33.b.3.1., across the open.

   ....(c)

-2-

(c) Aviation.

NIL.

3. HOSTILE DEFENCES.

Work and New Trenches.

Maintenance work only was observed to be in progress.
A working party were seen all morning in FARM TRENCH between G.14.a.2.2. and G.13.b.9.7. - about 2 men in each fire-bay. The men had no equipment on and the majority wore caps with a very light-coloured band.

4. MISCELLANEOUS.

(i) An enemy balloon was up near NAUROY, 9.10 - 9.40 a.m.
(ii) The suspected M.G. at ELEVEN TREES did not fire.
(iii) Our aircraft were heavily fired on by M.G's from about PEG COPSE.
(iv) A small party, with a machine gun and some Very pistols, are reported to move along BANK TRENCH at night. The M.G. fires bursts from several different points.

Captain,
G.S., Dismounted Divisions.

19th January, 1918.

CONFIDENTIAL.

SUMMARY OF INTELLIGENCE No. 30.

H.Q., DISMOUNTED DIVISIONS.

For 24 hours ending 6.0 a.m., 20/1/18.

1. **OPERATIONS.**

   Our Patrols.

   An Officer's patrol left our lines at 9.30 p.m. and reconnoitred FISHER'S CRATER and moved on to the N. But the moon was so bright that they came in. This patrol went out again at 12.30 a.m., moving along the S. side of SOMERVILLE WOOD to G.32.d.4.1., where they remained for half an hour. They report as follows:-
   (i) Working party was heard in direction of ELEVEN TREES.
   (ii) Small light seen N.E. of ELEVEN TREES at 12.0 midnight.
   (iii) Similar light seen in FISHER'S CRATER at 12.15 a.m.
   (iv) A rifle and a M.G. were fired from ST. HELENE TRENCH, while the moon was up.
   The patrol returned at 2.45 a.m.

   An Officer's patrol left DRAGOON POST at 6.0 p.m. and reconnoitred SOMERVILLE WOOD and DOG'S LEG, finding no sign of the enemy. The patrol reports as follows:-
   (i) 1 row of concertina wire, with trip wire running through it, runs from G.32.c.4.4. to G.32.c.4.8.
   (ii) Single strand of barbed wire, breast high, runs through S. edge of SOMERVILLE WOOD.
   (iii) A trip wire runs E. and W. between SOMERVILLE WOOD and DOG'S LEG.
   Owing to bright moonlight, patrol could not go further afield and returned to our line at 8.0 p.m.

   A patrol, also, reconnoitred the enemy's wire in front of BANK TRENCH, about G.8.c.2.8. and G.8.c.3.7.

2. **HOSTILE ATTITUDE AND ACTIVITY.**

   (a) *Artillery.*

   Enemy's activity against our Centre Sector was much below normal.
   Slight shelling of the following localities was reported during the day:- BERTHAUCOURT, R.10.b. and d., TUMULUS.

   11.45 a.m. 2 guns located firing from about G.34.c.6.3. This was reported to F.O.O. and our 4.5 hows. engaged the enemy guns.
   3.35 p.m.   1 gun located firing from same place and engaged by our hows.
   4.15 p.m.   15 4.2's fell in M.9.c., 6 of which were "blind."

   (b) *Movement.*

   The usual movement was seen in the forward area:
   8.40 a.m. Continual movement on skyline at G.14.a.0.5. which died down as daylight increased. Some of the men seen were carrying food containers.
   9.15 a.m. 3 men, carrying shovels, left QUILL TRENCH at G.33.b.5.5. and walked along parados to ST. HELENE TRENCH at G.33.c.9.0., where they commenced work on what appeared to be a M.G. emplacement. They worked here until 10.20 a.m., when they went into trench at G.33.d.1.6.

   ....9.30 a.m.

-2-

9.30 a.m.	Clouds of smoke seen coming from SWAN WORK.
12.10 p.m.	2 men at G.14.a.2.2. watched our line about HETTY POST for 15 minutes, one man using glasses. Both men were officers or "unter-offiziers", as they wore peaked caps.
1.10 p.m.	12 men, coming from BELLICOURT direction, carried timber and shovels to small mound at G.8.c.6.4.
1.30 p.m.	2 men at G.33.b.1.8. viewed our line through glasses for 5 minutes.
2.10 p.m.	13 men, with picks and shovels, left SWAN WORK and moved S. along top of QUILL TRENCH, disappearing at G.33.b.4.3.
2.45 p.m.	1 man, walking from M.3.b.1.7. to M.3.a.8.8., apparently hit by sniper from PONTRUET direction, as he fell and lay on the ground for 10 minutes.
3.40 p.m.	2 men, probably officers, seen pointing with sticks and reading maps, at G.27.a.9.4.

(c) Aviation.

9.50 a.m.	7 E.A. (7,000 ft.) flew along our line in N. direction, under A.A. fire.
1.30 p.m.	2 E.A. (10,000 feet) over HARGICOURT.
3.30 p.m.	2 E.A. (12,000 ") " "
4.15 p.m.	1 E.A. (5,000 ") over VILLERET, driven N.N.E. by A.A. fire.
4.30 p.m.	2 E.A., flying high towards LE VERGUIER, driven off by A.A. fire.

3. HOSTILE DEFENCES.

(a) Work and New Trenches.

(i) New trench is reported running E.S.E. from PINK TRENCH (about G.21.c.1.8. to G.21.c.5.6.). Confirmation by air photo required.
(ii) New trench, also, reported N. of the road in M.4.a.
(iii) 12 men seen working between G.28.c.8.8. and G.28.d.0.6., probably deepening the shallow trench in G.28.d.
(iv) Usual maintenance work observed to be in progress.

(b) Wire.

Vide para 1 above.
Gaps in enemy's wire reported at following points:- G.21.c.3.0., G.21.c.6.0., and G.27.a.6.5.

4. MISCELLANEOUS.

A.A. Guns.

2 A.A. guns seen to fire from sunk road G.3.b.0.1. - our artillery informed.

Very Lights.

At 5.30 a.m., 1 red and 1 white Very light were fired in quick succession from the same point. No action followed.

Enemy's Caps.

With very few exceptions, the Germans seen opposite our front are always wearing caps. Observers in our Right Sector report that these caps have a red band, with 2 very thin bands of white, above and below the red.

Captain,
G.S., Dismounted Divisions.

20th January, 1918.

Appendix 1

CONFIDENTIAL.   SUMMARY OF INTELLIGENCE No. 31.

H.Q., DISMOUNTED DIVISIONS.

For 24 hours ending 6.0 a.m. 21/1/18.

1. OPERATIONS.

   (a) Our Patrols.

   An Officer's patrol reconnoitred the shell-hole post at G.19.d.8.8., formerly an enemy L.P. No sign of any enemy was seen.

   The patrol, which reconnoitred the enemy's wire in front of BANK TRENCH on the night 19/20th, reported as follows:-
   (i) Gap in enemy wire about G.8.c.2.7. This is evidently used, as there is a distinct track through it.
   (ii) Sentry seen standing a few yards N. of this gap.
   (iii) There appeared to be 2 M.G's in the trench, the Northern one being located about G.8.c.1.9.

   (b) Our M.G's and T.M's.

   Our M.G's fired 2,000 rounds harassing fire at 8.25 p.m. and 9.10 p.m. at LA HAUTE BRUYERE. They, also, fired 2,000 rounds at 9.50 p.m. and 10.20 p.m. at BUISSON GAULAINE FM. and at TRENCH TRIANGLE (G.20.a.8.9.).
   Our T.M's fired 15 rounds retaliation on enemy front line in G.8.c.2.8. during the night.

2. HOSTILE ATTITUDE AND ACTIVITY.

   (a) Artillery.

   An increase of activity was reported against our forward area.
   6.45 - 7.30 a.m.   Heavy shelling between RAILWAY TRENCH and RAILWAY SUPPORT - 7.7's, 4.2's and 5.9's. VILLERET also shelled with 4.2's.
   10.15 - 12.15 a.m. Area M.1., M.7., and R.12. shelled with 4.2's.
   10.15 - 10.30 a.m. Heavy shelling of BARRIER POST (M.2.c.).
   Otherwise very slight shelling of PONTRU, RED WOOD, ASCENSION FM., L.10.c.0.0. and VILLERET.

   (b) Movement.

   Movement was normal in the forward area. Movement was seen in BANK TRENCH throughout the day - latterly, no movement has been seen here in the daytime. The enemy still walks across the open in G.14.a., where his trenches appear to be in a very bad state.
   8.5 a.m.   1 cart (like a Maltese cart) went from G.22.d.4.5. to G.28.a.8.9., where it was lost to view. It returned on same track at 9.30 a.m.
   10.25 a.m. 3 men left trench at G.20.d.8.7., carrying a M.G. and ammunition boxes. They moved across the open to G.20.b.9.0.
   10.30 a.m. 3 men looked through field-glasses at our line in G.7.b., from BANK TRENCH (G.1.d.05.20.). They continued to observe our line until 4.45 p.m. and were frequently visited by an Officer or N.C.O. All wore caps with white bands.
   11.30 a.m. to 12 Noon.   20 men, moving 2 at a time and carrying food containers, moved down road from G.34.d.5.5. to G.34.d.1.1.

   ....2.10 p.m

- 2 -

2.10 p.m. Artillery observer reported to be observing for enemy's fire on VILLERET from G.14.a.2.1.

(c) Aviation.

9.15 a.m. 4 E.A. (12,000 ft.) circled over VILLERET.

10.45 a.m. 5 E.A. (very high) passed over COTE WOOD and then turned off S.E. under A.A. fire.

11.30 a.m. 6 E.A. (very high) flew towards PRIEL FARM but driven off by A.A. fire.

11.55 a.m. 7 E.A. (11,000 ft.) flew over RAILWAY TRENCH and back again.

3. HOSTILE DEFENCES.

(a) Work and New Trenches.

The following maintenance work was seen to be in progress:-

8.50 a.m. Mud being thrown out of PINK TRENCH (G.27.a.8.8.) for 10 minutes.

9.45 a.m. Mud being thrown out of trench at G.33.d.9.1. for 5 minutes.

9.50 a.m. Man working trench-pump on parapet at G.20.b.3.5. for 15 minutes.

Earth continually being thrown from ONOTO TRENCH about G.33.d.1.7. during the day.

Earth also being thrown out of BANK TRENCH about G.8.a.0.3.

(b) Wire.

At 8.30 a.m., 3 men left trench at G.33.d.6.8. and were wiring for 10 minutes G.33.d.3.0.

Gap in enemy's wire reported at M.3.c.9.5. This confirms former observer's report - vide Summary No.20, para. 3 (b).

4. HOSTILE ORGANIZATION.

(a) Railways.

An engine was seen on light railway at G.22.a.4.5. and lost to view at G.22.c.1.9.

(b) Communications.

At 8.45 p.m., a lamp was seen signalling from N.W. corner of NAUROY. The lamp was set facing W.

5. MISCELLANEOUS.

Enemy's A.A. guns again active from G.3.b.0.1.

Several fires seen during night some distance behind enemy's lines, in an E. and N.E. direction.

W. Browne, Captain,
G.S., Dismounted Divisions.

21st January, 1918.

Appendix 1

CONFIDENTIAL.

SUMMARY OF INTELLIGENCE NO. 32.

H.Q., DISMOUNTED DIVISIONS.

For 24 hours ending 6.0 a.m. 22/1/18.

1. OPERATIONS.

   (a) Our Patrols.

   An Officer's patrol left our line at 1.45 a.m. and reconnoitred FISHER'S CRATER, which they found unoccupied. The patrol went forward to M.3.c.6.4. An enemy M.G. was firing from about M.3.d.5.9. From here, the patrol leader and one man went on to M.3.c.8.6., where they found a gap in the wire across the road. They went through this gap and up to the trench but could see no sign of any occupants. As daylight was approaching, the patrol-leader rejoined his patrol and returned to our line at 6.0 a.m.

   An Officer's patrol reconnoitred the enemy's wire in front of BANK TRENCH and reports a large gap in the wire at G.7.b.8.9. The enemy was very alert. An enemy M.G. was located firing from about G.7.b.9.5.

   (b) Enemy's Patrols.

   An enemy patrol, about 8 strong, was seen coming from RAILWAY CUTTING (G.8.c.2.4.) towards our wire. They were dispersed by our fire.

   (c) Our M.G's and T.M's.

   Our M.G's fired 4,000 rounds harassing fire between 9.30 and 10.15 p.m. on the following targets:- 2,000 rounds on QUARRY, G.14.central; 2,000 rounds on tracks in G.15.a.
   Our T.M's fired 47 rounds retaliation during the day with good effect.

2. HOSTILE ATTITUDE AND ACTIVITY.

   (a) Artillery:

   Normal activity. Slight shelling of BARRIER POST, TUMULUS, MARTEN POST, COPE WOOD and L.10.d.
   12.0 noon.   12 4.2's fell in L.16.b.
   2.40 - 3.25 p.m. 9 rounds from H.V. gun burst at L.30.c.9.5. Gun appeared to be firing from about G.28.a.2.7.
   3.20 p.m.   4 shells burst in SOMERVILLE WOOD.
   5.30 - 5.45 p.m. 30 4.2's fell on railway about L.12.a.0.7.

   (b) Enemy M.G's and T.M's.

   Enemy M.G. fired on BERTHAUCOURT and LONE TREE POST at intervals during night, and on DRAGOON POST at 9.10 p.m. A M.G. was seen, mounted on a high pole at G.34.c.0.2. At 5.45 a.m., M.G's reported firing from G.8.a.0.3. and G.8.c.2.9.
   Enemy T.M's fired 40 rounds between RAILWAY TRENCH and SUPPORT at 9.30 a.m., and 10 6" T.M. bombs fell about G.7.d.5.0. at 10.50 a.m.
   68 rifle grenades burst near TURNIP LANE and FARM SUPPORT at 10.30 a.m.

   (c) Enemy Movement.

   Visibility was poor until 3.30 p.m. The usual movement was observed along the whole of the front trench system, except in BANK TRENCH, where no movement was seen. Enemy's trenches are still in very

   ......bad

-2-

bad state in G.14.a., and all traffic here is across the open.

7.26 a.m.   12 men, with 2 M.G's, seen at G.21.a.9.6.; 6 of them walked across open to G.27.a.8.5.;remainder walked to G.21.a.central and disappeared from view.

7.45 a.m.   2 men at G.1.d.9.3, observing our left with glasses and periscope throughout the day. Neither man wore equipment, one had peaked cap. vide Summary No. 31, para. 2(b)

9.30 a.m.   8 men entered WAT TRENCH, G.27.c.9.5. from WATLING STREET.

10.30 a.m. 4 men, carrying food containers and followed by 2 more carrying dicksee on pole, walked along top of trench from M.4.a.3.6. to M.3.b.6.8., where lost to view. There seems to be a dug-out here, as other men were seen coming to and fro' with dicksees.

12.27 p.m. 4 men, working trench pump at G.27.a.5.8.

Considerable movement reported during day between WATLING STREET and trench at G.27.c.9.5.
Observers suspect a cook-house in trench G.21.c.6.1. - G.21.c.3.0.
Exit from LING ALLEY at G.27.b.6.0. is much used.

(d) Aviation.

No E.A. activity. A special report has been rendered to Cavalry Corps re aeroplanes with British markings, which are suspected of being enemy machines.

3. HOSTILE DEFENCES.

(a) Work and New Trenches.

New earth was seen along trenches at the following points:-
     At G.27.a.8.8.
     Between G.21.c.1.6. and G.21.c.2.3.
     "   G.21.c.0.9. " G.20.b.8.2. where 11 men were working during morning.
A large hole appears to have been dug about M.3.d.4.4.
4 men were seen digging at G.27.b.1.6. in afternoon.

(b) Wire.

2 parties of 5 men each seen wiring about G.14.a.1.1. and G.14.c.2.8. at 7.5 a.m. They withdrew to Quarry (G.14.a.8.7.) when light improved.
Reference Summary No. 30, para.1 (a), the row of concertina wire reported running from G.32.c.4.4. to G.32.c.4.6. is thought to be an isolated strand of old wire.
Reference Summary No.30, para.3 (b), observers reported that the 3 gaps in enemy's wire were closed on the morning of the 20th (i.e. at G.21.c.3.0., G.21.c.6.0. and G.27.a.6.5.)

4. HOSTILE ORGANIZATION.

Communications.

8.5 a.m.   3 men apparently inspecting ground line at G.20.d.9.3.
8.10 a.m.   2 linesmen repairing rocking stay-wire on post at G.21.c.0.2.
9.5 a.m.   4 men seen with drum of cable at G.21.a.0.3.
9.37 a.m.   3 men inspected telephone cable at G.27.d.9.5.
1.28 p.m.   1 man repairing line behind trench at G.21.c.7.3.

5. MISCELLANEOUS.

4.0 p.m.   Green lights, bursting into 3 and sometimes 8 white lights, were seen S.E. of PONTRUET.

Captain,
G.S., Dismounted Divisions.

22nd January, 1918.

SECRET.

G.842
7/1/18.

3rd Dismounted Division.
A.D.M.S.

1. Reference this office G.667/35 dated 6/1/18, on the relief of the 3rd Dismounted Division a party of approximately 600 other ranks will remain behind for work in the forward area.

2. The party will be known as the 3rd Cav. Div. Pioneer Regiment consisting of Headquarters and 3 squadrons, each squadron being formed from the 3 regiments in each Dismounted Brigade (squadron strength 200 other ranks).

3. Headquarters will be composed as follows:-

        C.O.   a Field Officer.
        Adjutant.
        Quarter-Master.
        A/R.S.M.
        A/R.Q.M.S.
        Orderly Room Clerk.
        Cook.
        M.O. and Medical Personnel.

The above Headquarters will be detailed by the G.O.C. 3rd Dismounted Division with the exception of medical personnel who will be detailed by A.D.M.S.

4. A squadron will consist of

        1 Major or Captain.
        4 Subalterns.
        6 Sergeants.
        6 Corporals.
        About 180 other ranks.

5. The above Pioneer Regiment will move to the area of the 8th Cavalry Division on relief of the 3rd Dismounted Division under orders which will be issued later.

6. Details as to transport will be issued later.

7. It is intended to relieve the personnel of this Pioneer Regiment by personnel from the back area as early as possible after the return of the 3rd Dismounted Division.

                              Lieutenant-Colonel,
                        G.S., Dismounted Divisions,

7th January 1918.

Copy, for information, to
        Cavalry Corps,
        8th Cavalry Division.
        Q.
        Signals, Dismounted Divisions.
        6th Cavalry Brigade.
        7th Cavalry Brigade.
        8th Cavalry Brigade.

SECRET.

3rd Dismounted Division.
6th Cavalry Brigade.
3rd Cav. Div. "Q".
A.A. & Q.M.G., Dismtd. Divs.

Appendix 3

5/1/18.

1. Headquarters, 3rd Dragoon Guards will relieve Headquarters, North Somerset Yeomanry as Headquarters, 6th Dismounted Brigade on January 8th.

2. Relieving party less mounted details will proceed by rail to ROISEL, to reach there by 1 p.m. on January 8th, under arrangements to be made by 6th Cavalry Brigade.

North Somerset Yeomanry party on relief, less mounted details, will proceed to back area by rail under arrangements to be made by 3rd Dismounted Division.

3. Mounted details of each party will move in accordance with March Table overleaf.

4. All parties will be rationed up to and including the day following day of arrival at final destination.

5. Acknowledge.

5th January, 1918.

Captain,
G.S., Dismounted Divisions.

MARCH TABLE:

Serial No.	Unit.	Date.	From.	To.	Route.	Remarks.
		1918.				
1.	Mounted details, 3rd Dragoon Guards.	Jan. 7th.	AILLY LE HAUT CLOCHER area.	LAMOTTE en SANTERRE.	Any.	Billets from Maire.
2.	do.	" 8th.	LAMOTTE en SANTERRE.	Wagon Lines, VERMAND.	Any.	Billets from 3rd Dismounted Division.
3.	Mounted details, North Somerset Yeomanry	" 9th.	Wagon lines, VERMAND.	LAMOTTE en SANTERRE.	Any.	Billets from Maire.
4.	do.	" 10th.	LAMOTTE en SANTERRE.	LONG - EPOILE area.	Any.	Billets from 6th Cavalry Brigade.

Appendix 4

S E C R E T.　　　　　　　　　　　　　　　　　　　　　　　Copy No.......

DISMOUNTED DIVISIONS ORDER NO. 2.

1.　　The 3rd. Dismounted Division will be relieved in the line (Right Sector) by the 5th. Dismounted Division. Reliefs will be completed by the 15th. January.

2.　　Reliefs will be carried out in accordance with the attached table.

3.　　Intervals of 200 yards will be observed between Squadrons and similar units.

4.　　On completion of relief troops of 3rd. Dismounted Division (less 3rd. Field Squadron) will move to back area by rail with the exception of a Pioneer Regiment 600 strong which will remain in the forward area for work, and be accommodated at TREMOON.

5.　　The C.R.E. Dismounted Divisions will arrange direct with the C.R.E. 5th. Cavalry Division for the relief of the 3rd. Field Squadron by the 5th. Field Squadron. 3rd. Field Squadron on relief will move to ATHIES.

6.　　The A.D.M.S. Dismounted Divisions will arrange direct with the A.D.M.S. 5th. Cavalry Division regarding the relief of R.A.M.C. units.

7.　　All details of relief not provided for in this order will be arranged mutually between B.G's C. concerned.

8.　　No artillery reliefs will take place.

9.　　All trench stores, Aeroplane photos, Defence Schemes, Trench Maps and Sketches etc., will be handed over and receipts obtained.

10.　　Command of Right Sector will pass to G.O.C. 5th. Dismounted Division on completion of relief.

11.　　Major-General Macandrew, C.B., D.S.O., and Staff will relieve Major-General Vaughan, C.B., D.S.O., and Staff in command of the Dismounted Divisions in Right and Centre Sector on completion of relief of the 3rd. Dismounted Division by the 5th. Dismounted Division. Command will pass at 10 a.m. on 16th. January.

12.　　Details as to entrainment and movement of dismounted details will be issued later.

13.　　Acknowledge.

　　　　　　　　　　　　　　　　　　　　　　　　　　　Major, G.S.,
10th. January, 1918.　　　　　　　Dismounted Divisions.

Copies to :-

No. 1.	2nd. Dismtd. Divn.	11.	A.P.M.
2.	3rd. Dismtd. Divn.	12.	Divl. Gas Officer.
3.	Cav. Divl. Arty.	13.	French Liaison Officer.
4.	C.R.E. Dismtd. Divns.	14.	6th. Cav. Bde.
5.	Divl. M.G.O.	15.	7th. Cav. Bde.
6.	Signals Dismtd. Divns.	16.	8th. Cav. Bde.
7.	"Q" Dismtd. Divns.	17.	5th. French Division.
8.	"Q" 3rd. Cav. Div.	18.	24th. Division.
9.	A.D.M.S.	19.	Cavalry Corps.
10.	A.D.V.S.	20.	Cavalry Corps H.A.

Table of Reliefs issued with Dismounted Divisions Order No. 2.

1. Serial No.	2. Date.	3. Unit to be relieved.	4. To be relieved by.	5. Advance Parties.	6.	7. Remarks.
1.	Jan. 13th.			Advance parties 5th. Dismtd.Divn. Machine Guns to reconnoitre dispositions reporting at 3rd. Dismtd. Divn. H.Q. at 3 P.M.	3rd.Dismtd.Divn. Units moving after relief to	
2.	Jan. 14th.			Advance parties of Reserve Dismtd. Bde. 5th. Dismtd. Divn. report, parties of 1 Regt. at FORT DYCE, LE VERGUIER (L.34.a. 3.6.) & parties of remainder of Bde. at VADENCOURT at H.Q. Res. Dismtd. Bde. both at 9 a.m.		
3.	Jan. 14th.			Advance parties of Dismtd. Bdes. of 5th Dismtd. Divn. taking over front & support lines in A.1 & A.2. sub-sectors to report to respective sub-sector H.Q. at 4 p.m.		H.Q. of A.1. & A.2. sub-sector are at R.11.c.8.8. & L.28.c.2.1. respectively.
4.	Night 14/15	All Machine Guns 3rd. Dismtd. Divn.	All Machine Guns 5th. Dismtd. Divn.		VENDELLES where they will be conveyed by light railway to ROISEL & entrain for back area on night 14/15th.	Details of relief to be arranged by Divl.M.G.Offr. Dismtd.Divns.

(contd..)

1 Serial No.	2 Date.	3 Unit to be relieved.	4 To be relieved by.	5 Advanced Parties.	6 3rd.Dismtd.Divn. unit moving after relief to	7 Remarks.
5.	Night 14/15	Res.Dismtd Bde.(less 1 Regt.) at VADEN-COURT & 1 Regt. Res. Dismtd. Bde. at LE VERGUIE.	Similar unit 5th. Dismtd. Divn.		VENDELLES when they will be conveyed at 9 p.m. by Light Railway to ROISEL for entrainment to back area.	Units of 5th.Dis. Divn. to arrive at places as in Col. 3 at 4.30 p.m. 14th. Jan.
6.	Night 15/16	Dismtd. Bdes of 3rd. Dismtd. Divn. in front line in A.1 & A.2 sub-sectors.	- do -		VENDELLES whence they will be conveyed at 10 p.m. by light railway to ROISEL for entrainment to back area.	Units of 5th. Dis. Divn. to arrive as follows at 4 p.m. on 15th. Units for A.1 Sub Sector. BIHECOURT Cross-roads R.21.b.9.8. Units for A.2 Sub Sector. Western entrance to LE VERGUIER on JEANCOURT road.
7.	Jan. 15th.	3rd. Field Sqdn.	- do -		ATHIES.	Billets from 4th. Cav. Div.
8.	"	7th. Cav. Fd. Amb.	- do -		Back area by road.	Relief to be completed by 10 a.m. Dismtd. personnel will entrain under orders of 3rd. Dismtd. Divn
9.	"	Transport of Serial Nos. 4. & 5.			-do-	
10.	Jan. 13th.	Transport of Serial No. 6.			-do-	

Appendix 5

S E C R E T.   10th. January, 1918.

WARNING   ORDER.

1.   Reference Dismounted Divisions Order No. 2. of 10th. inst.

2.   Pending the issue of fresh orders, the following amendments will be made to the above quoted order, and table attached thereto.

   (a) "1st. Dismounted Division" will be substituted for "5th. Dismounted Division" throughout the order.

   (b) Para 5. last sentence.

       3rd. Field Squadron on relief will move to 1st. Cavalry Division Area.

   (c) Para. 11.

       Major-General R.L. MULLENS, C.B. and Staff will be substituted for Major-General H.J.M. MACANDREW, C.B., D.S.O. and Staff.

   (d) Para 11.

       Command will pass at a time to be notified later on January 23rd.

3. Acknowledge

Issued at 10 p.m.

                                                         Major,
                                            G.S., Dismounted Divisions.

Copies to :-

   No. 1. 2nd. Dismtd. Divn.   11. A.P.M.
       2. 3rd. Dismtd. Divn.   12. D.G.O.
       3. Cav. Divl. Artillery.   13. French Liaison Officer.
       4. C.R.E. Dismtd. Divns.   14. 6th. Cav. Bde.
       5. Divl. M.G.O.   15. 7th. Cav. Bde.
       6. Signals Dismtd. Divns.   16. 8th. Cav. Bde.
       7. "A" Dismtd. Divns.   17. 5th. French Division. for info
       8. "Q" 3rd. Cav. Div.   18. 24th. Division.
       9. A.D.M.S.   19. Cavalry Corps.
      10. A.D.V.S.   20. Cavalry Corps H.A.
                                      21. 1st   "   "
                                      22. 5th   "   "

Operations 6

S E C R E T.

2nd Dismounted Division.
24th Division.
3rd Dismounted Division.)
A.A. & Q.M.G., Dismtd.Divs.) for information.
2nd Cavalry Division.   )
Cavalry Corps.   )

G.667/46.
12/1/18.

1. Composite L.T.M. Battery (2nd and 3rd Cavalry Divisions) will relieve 73rd L.T.M. Battery in Centre Sector on the night 15/16th instant. Relief to be completed by 8 a.m. 16th instant, under orders of 2nd Dismounted Division.

2. On relief 73rd L.T.M. Battery will be withdrawn under orders issued by 24th Division.

3. Composite L.T.M. Battery will move by lorry from back area of 2nd Cavalry Division to MONTIGNY FM. on 14th instant, where they will be met and accommodated under arrangements to be made by 2nd Dismounted Division. Move to be completed by 4 p.m.

4. By arrangements with 24th Division, Lieut. SMITH, 73rd L.T.M. Battery, is available to remain in line with Composite L.T.M. Battery until 4 p.m. 16th instant.

5. Completion of relief will be reported to Dismounted Divisions and repeated 24th Division.

12th January, 1918.

Major,
G.S., Dismounted Divisions.

S E C R E T.   Copy No. ....

DISMOUNTED DIVISIONS ORDER No. 3.

13th January, 1918.

1.   3rd Dismounted Division on relief, less 3rd Field Squadron and 7th Cavalry Field Ambulance, will move to the DOMART-en-PONTHIEU AREA by rail and road in accordance with Tables "A" and "B" attached.

2.   Units moving by rail will be conveyed from Detraining Points under arrangements to be made by A/D.A.A. & Q.M.G., 3rd Cavalry Division.

3.   Parties moving by road will march as Brigade parties and will observe intervals of 200 yards between Brigade parties.

4.   3rd Field Squadron on relief by 1st Field Squadron will move independently on 15th to FLAMICOURT where they will be accommodated by 1st Cavalry Division.

5.   7th Cavalry Field Ambulance will be disposed under the orders of A.D.M.S. Dismounted Divisions.

6.   Dismounted Brigades and detached details will be concentrated at entraining points on light railways under orders of 3rd Dismounted Division.

7.   Parties will be rationed up to and including the day following day of arrival at final destination.

8.   Acknowledge.

Issued at .....8.9..P.M.

                                                       Major,
                                            G.S., Dismounted Divisions.

Copies to:-
   No. 1. 3rd Dismounted Division.   No. 8. A.D.M.S.,Dismtd.Divns.
       2. A.A. & Q.M.G.,Dismtd.Divs.   9. S.S.O.,   "   "
       3. 3rd Cav. Div. "Q".   10. 24th Divn.)
       4. D.M.G.O.   11. 61st   "   ) for
       5. Cav. Div. Artillery.   12. 1st Cav.Div.)information
       6. C.R.E., Dismtd. Divns.   13. Cav. Corps.)
       7. Signals,   "   "   14. 2nd Dismtd. Div.
                                               15. D. G. O.
                                               16. 6th Cav. Bde.
                                               17. 7th   "   "
                                               18. 8th   "   "
                                               19. Cav. Corps H.A.

TABLE "A" — Issued with Dismounted Divisions Order No. 3.

Serial No.	Unit.	Off.	O.R.	Date.	Entrain light railway.	Time.	Entrain normal gauge.	Detrain.
1.	8th Dismounted Bde.	17	394	Night 14/15	VENDELLES.	9.0 p.m.	ROISEL.	VIGNACOURT.
2.	6th, 7th & 8th M.G. Squadrons.	15	221	"	do.	9.0 p.m.	do.	do.
3.	H.Q., 3rd Dismounted Division.	4	20	15/16	do.	10.0 p.m.	do.	LONGPRÉ.
4.	6th Dismounted Bde.	17	375	"	do.	10.0 p.m.	do.	do.
5.	7th " "	15	414	"	do.	10.0 p.m.	do.	do.

Note Trains will leave ROISEL about 1 hour after arrival of Light Ry Train.

TABLE "B" - Issued with Dismounted Divisions Order No. 3.

Serial No.	Unit.	Date.	From.	To.	Route.	Remarks.
1.	Mounted Details, 8th Dismtd. Brigade.	Jan. 15th.	Wagon Lines, VERKAND	FRAMERVILLE.	Any.	Billets as under:— FRAMERVILLE:— From Area bounded South, VILLERS BRETONNEUX.
2.	Mounted Details, 6th,7th & 8th M.G.Squadrons.	"	do.	do.	"	
3.	As for Serial 1.	16th	FRAMERVILLE.	CAMON.	"	CAMON:— From Moreuil
4.	" " " 2.	"	do.	do.	"	
5.	Mounted Details, 6th Dismtd. Brigade.	"	Wagon Lines, VERKAND	FRAMERVILLE.	"	
6.	Mounted Details, 7th Dismtd. Brigade.	"	do.	do.	"	
7.	Details, 3rd Cav. Rgs. Park.	"	do.	do.	"	
8.	As for Serial 1.	17th	CAMON.	VIGNACOURT area.	"	(a) All troops to pass round Northern outskirts of AMIENS.
9.	" " " 2.	"	do.	Respective Brigade areas.	"	(b) No troops to be billeted in:—
10.	" " " 5.	"	FRAMERVILLE.	CAMON.	"	HALLOY les PERNOIS.
11.	" " " 6.	"	do.	do.	"	CANAPLES.
12.	" " " 7.	"	do.	do.	"	FRANQUEVILLE. PERNOIS.
13.	" " " 5.	18th.	CAMON.	AILLY le HAUT CLOCHER area.	"	FIEFFES.
14.	" " " 6.	"	do.	FRANSU area.	"	
15.	" " " 7.	"	do.	Area MONTRELET & FIENVILLERS.	"	

SECRET.

Appendix 8

6th Cavalry Brigade.	A.D.M.S., Dismtd.Divs.
7th Cavalry Brigade.	S.S.O. " "
8th Cavalry Brigade.	D.G.O. " "
3rd Cav. Pioneer Regiment.	3rd Cav. Div. "Q".
A.A. & Q.M.G., Dismtd.Divs.	

G.842/6
16/1/18

1.   Reference G.842 of 7th instant.

2.   Brigades will detail reliefs for 3rd Cavalry Pioneer Regiment as shewn in attached table.

3.   First relief will be carried out as soon as possible after arrival of 3rd Dismounted Division in the back area. Reliefs will be ready to move at any time after 18th instant.

4.   Transport will not be relieved.

5.   Medical Officers and personnel will be detailed and reliefs carried out under order of A.D.M.S., Dismounted Divisions.

6.   Orders as to date of relief and move will be issued later.

7.   For the present the 3rd Cavalry Pioneer Regiment will be located as under:-

    Headquarters and 2 Squadrons   ...   VENDELLES.
    1 Squadron   ...   .   BIHECOURT and TREFCON.

8.   Acknowledge.

                                           Major,
16th January, 1918.   G.S., Dismounted Divisions.

Table of Reliefs of 3rd Cavalry Pioneer Regiment, issued with Mounted Divisions G.812/6 dated 18.1.18.

Serial No.	Unit.	Headquarters.		Pioneer Squadrons.				Transport.	Remarks.
				Off.	Sgts.	Cpls.	R.& F.(1)		
1.	6th Cav. Bde.	Adjutant. A/R.Q.M. Cook.	1 1 1	4(a)	3	6	171	3 L.G.S. Wagons.	(a) 1 Major or Capt. 3 subalterns.
2.	7th Cav. Bde.	O.C. (Field Offr.) A/R.Q.M.S. Cook Sergt.	1 1 1	5(b)	8	8	228(c)	4 L.G.S. Wagons. (includes 1 for H.Q.)	(b) 1 Major or Capt. 4 subalterns. (c) 120 O.R. including Sgts. and Cpls. from 2nd Life Guards.
3.	8th Cav. Bde.	Quartermaster. J.R. Clerk. Transport Sgt.	1 1 1	4(a)	5	6	171	3 L.G.S. Wagons. 1 Mess Cart. 1 Water Cart.	(a) 1 Major or Capt. 3 subalterns.

(d) These numbers do not include cooks, servants or sanitary men, or drivers.

Appendix 9

```
SECRET.
2nd Dismounted Division.         A.D.V.S.
1st Dismounted Division.         A.P.M.
A.A. & Q.M.G., Dismtd.Divns.     D.G.O.
3rd Cav. Div. "Q".               6th Cav. Bde.
D.M.G.O.                         7th Cav. Bde.
Cav. Div. Artillery.             8th Cav. Bde.
C.R.E., Dismtd. Divns.           61st Division.              G.992
Signals    "        "            24th Division.              20/1/18.
A.D.M.S.   "        "            Cavalry Corps.
S.S.O.     "        "            Cavalry Corps H.A.
```

1. Reference Dismounted Divisions Order No. 2 and Warning Order of January 10th.

2. Command of Dismounted Divisions will pass to G.O.C. 1st Cavalry Division at 10 a.m. 23rd instant.

3. Divisional Headquarters will move on 23rd instant to the area DOMART-en-PONTHIEU.

4. There will be no Artillery reliefs.

5. Mounted Details will proceed in accordance with Table overleaf, rationed up to and including January 25th.

6. Acknowledge.

20th January, 1918.

Major,
G.S., Dismounted Divisions.

MARCH TABLE.
==*=*=*=*=*=*=*=*=*=*

Serial No.	Unit.	Date.	From	To	Route	Remarks
1.	Mounted Details, H.Q., 3rd Cav. Div.	Jan. 23rd	BOUVINCOURT.	LAMOTTE-en-SANTERRE	Any	Billets from 12th Pontoon Park for 2 Off. 60 O.R. and 60 horses.
2.	3rd Signal Squadron.	"	do.	do.	"	
3.	As for Serial 1.	24th	LAMOTTE-en-SANTERRE.	DOMART-en-PONTHIEU	"	Camp Commandant, 3rd Cav. Div.
4.	" " " 2.	"	do.	do.	"	

S E C R E T.   Appendix 10

                    Warning Order.

                                                    24th January, 1918.

1.   The Division will be concentrated in the present area of 5th Cavalry Division (MONCHY LAGACHE) by February 1st.

2.   Move will be carried out in 2 stages by Brigade Groups commencing on 27th instant as under. Staging area PROYART.

     8th Cavalry Brigade will move on 27th.
     6th   "   "   "   " 28th to 8th Cav. Bde. area.
     7th   "   "   "   " 30th "   "   "   "   "

3.   Detailed orders will be issued later.

4.   Acknowledge.

                                                           Major,
                                            G.S., 3rd Cavalry Division.

Issued at   4.15   p.m.

6th Cavalry Brigade.   A.D.M.S.
7th Cavalry Brigade.   A.D.V.S.
8th Cavalry Brigade.   A.P.M.
3rd Cav. Pioneer Regt.   O.C. A.S.C.
4th Bde. R.H.A.   Camp Commandant.
3rd Fd. Sqdn. R.E.   Field Cashier.
3rd Signal Squadron.   Cav. Corps.
3rd Cav. Reserve Park.   H.Q. L. of C.
A.A. & Q.M.G.   D.A.D.O.S.
                                3rd Cav Div School.

SECRET.   Copy No........

3rd. CAVALRY DIVISION ORDER NO. 14.

Ref. Map. 1/100,000.
Sheet LENS. 11.   25th. January, 1918.
   "   AMIENS. 17.
   "   ST. QUENTIN 13.

1.   3rd. Cavalry Division less 4th. Bde. R.H.A., 3rd. Field Sqdn. R.E. and 3rd. Cav. Pioneer Regt. will be concentrated in the MONCHY LAGACHE Area (now occupied by 5th. Cavalry Division) by February 1st. in accordance with March Table overleaf. The 5th. Cavalry Division will move into the Area now occupied by 3rd. Cavalry Division by February 2nd.

2.   Brigades will close up in the present 8th. Cavalry Brigade Area under Brigade arrangements.

3.   Intervals of 200 yards will be observed between Squadrons and similar units.

4.   Brigades will arrange to reconnoitre PROYART Area forthwith, in consultation with Administrative Commandant, Back Area South, VILLERS BRETONNEUX.

5.   Dismounted details of 2nd. Life Guards will proceed under orders to be issued later.

6.   Parties detailed to proceed to Cavalry Corps Equitation School will remain in their present Brigade Areas and will move from there to CAYEUX sur MER under separate instructions.

7.   3rd. Cavalry Division Headquarters will close at DOMART en PONTHIEU at 12 noon on January 30th. opening at MONCHY LAGACHE at the same hour.

8.   Acknowledge.

                                                                                Major,
Issued at   5.0   p.m.   G.S. 3rd. Cavalry Division.

Copy No. 1. 6th. Cavalry Brigade.   10. A.D.M.S.
         2. 7th.   "   "   11. A.D.V.S.
         3. 8th.   "   "   12. A.P.M.
         4. 3rd. Cav. Pioneer Regt.   13. O.C. A.S.C.
         5. 4th. Bde. R.H.A.   14. Camp. Commandant.
         6. 3rd. Fd. Sqdn. R.E.   15. Field Cashier.
         7. 3rd. Signal Sqdn.   16. Cavalry Corps.
         8. 3rd. Cav. Res. Park.   17. H.Q. L. of C.
         9. A.A. & Q.M.G.   18. D.A.D.O.S.
                                            19. 3rd. Cav. Div. School.
                                            20. 5th Cav. Div.

MARCH TABLE ISSUED WITH 3RD. CAVALRY DIVISION ORDER NO. 14.

Serial No.	Unit.	Date.	From.	To.	Route.	Remarks.
1.	3rd. Cav. Res. Park.	Jan. 26th.	MONTRELET & FIENVILLERS	ST.LEGER les DOMART	No restrictions.	Under orders of A.A. & Q.M.G.
2.	8th. Cav. Bde.	27th.	BELLOY sur SOMME Area.	PROYART Area.	X roads ½ mile N. of Q in BERTRI-COURT – roads N. & E of CITADELLE in AMIENS – DAOURS ½ – FOUILLOY – WARFUSEE – ABANCOURT.	
3.	Serial 1.	"	ST.LEGER les DOMART.	"	"	Under orders of 8th Cav. Bde.
4.	Serials 1 & 2.	28th.	PROYART Area.	MÉRANCOURT Area.	FOUCAUCOURT – BRIE – ESTREES en CHAUSSEE.	Not to commence crossing bridges AT BRIE before 11.30 a.m.
5.	6th. Cav. Bde.	"	LONGUET Area.	BELLOY sur SOMME Area.	No restrictions.	PICQUIGNY, BREILLY & AILLY sur SOMME also available.
6.	Div. H.Q. details H.Q. A.S.C.; 3rd Signal Sqdn.	29th.	DOMART en PONTHIEU	PROYART Area.	FLESSELLES – VILLERS BOCAGE – QUERRIEU – DAOURS	Under orders of 6th. Cav. Bde.
7.	Serial 5.	"	BELLOY sur SOMME Area	"	As for Serial 2	
8.	Serials 5 & 6	30th.	PROYART Area.	TERTRY Area.	As for Serial 4.	As for Serial 4.
9.	7th. Cav. Bde	"	FRANSU Area.	BELLOY sur SOMME Area.	No restrictions.	Move to be completed by 11 am. PICQUIGNY, BREILLY, AILLY sur SOMME
10.	do.	31st.	BELLOY sur SOMME Area.	PROYART Area.	As for Serial 2	also available.
11.	do.	Feb. 1st.	PROYART Area.	TREFCON Area.	As for Serial 4	As for Serial 4.

www.ingramcontent.com/pod-product-compliance
Lightning Source LLC
Chambersburg PA
CBHW081242170426
43191CB00034B/2016